S0-AUM-602

SELECTED POEMS

ALSO BY DARA WIER

Remnants of Hannah

Reverse Rapture

Hat on a Pond

Voyages in English

Our Master Plan

Blue for the Plough

The Book of Knowledge

All You Have in Common

The 8-Step Grapevine

Blood, Hook & Eye

Limited Editions

Fly on the Wall

The Lost Epic of Arthur Davidson Ficke

X in Fix

Flawless

DARA WIER

SELECTED POEMS

WAVE BOOKS

SEATTLE · NEW YORK

Published by Wave Books
www.wavepoetry.com

Copyright © 2009 by Dara Wier
All rights reserved

Wave Books titles are distributed to the trade by
Consortium Book Sales and Distribution
Phone: 800-283-3572 / SAN 631-760X

Library of Congress Cataloging-in-Publication Data:
Wier, Dara, 1949–
   [Poems. Selections]
   Selected poems : 1977–2006 / Dara Wier.—1st ed.
      p. cm.
   ISBN 978-1-933517-38-4 (hardcover : alk. paper)
   I. Title.
PS3573.I357A6 2009
811'.54—dc22
                                        2009007455

Grateful acknowledgment to the original publishers and editors of the books from
which these poems have been selected and to the editors and publishers of journals,
paper and electronic, where many of these poems first were published. With
thanks to James Tate, Emily Pettit, Guy Pettit, Matthew Zapruder, Betsy Wheeler,
R.H.W. Dillard, Cathryn Hankla, David Madden, Franklin Holcomb, James Haug,
Alix Kennedy, Frank Bergon, Holly St. John, Valerie Martin, John Cullen, Monica
Fambrough and Brandon Shimoda for help with this book, and through the years.

Poems in sections one and two from *All You Have in Common, Blue for the Plough,
Our Master Plan,* and *Voyages in English* appear with the permission of Carnegie
Mellon University Press, www.cmu.edu/universitypress

Designed and composed by Gretchen Achilles/Wavetrap Design
Printed in the United States of America

9 8 7 6 5 4 3 2 1

FIRST EDITION

FOR EMILY AND GUY

FOR JIM

CONTENTS

FOUR

ONE

SHE HAS THIS PHANTOM LIMB

She tucks her arm limp as a doorknocker under her arm.
Now she has this phantom limb hidden in
an antique clarinet case, polished.
The days she practiced.
Next to her pink skin the red velvet thickens.
She paints the nails.
She oils the hand and thinks
it is moving
down some man's back.
She practices sign language.
She wants a reader.
Her palm is hard as antlers.
She buys deerskin gloves and slips
the bony fingers in.
She buys one ring, she buys two
and waits for spring
not noticing the noise,
the gold and bone.

THE DIRECTION TO THE LEFT OF SUNRISE

I've cut the circle, the globe's
Flat face, and laid it down: a coin
On a blackjack table.
Which way is up?

Have I been standing all these people
On their heads? Rushing the blood
To their brains. Rolling their bloodshot
Eyes up in jackpot rows.

The Northern Hemisphere holds my sky.
My girl scout compass could be pointing
South but isn't.
Why is it?

What *is* North?
What is central to our direction?
The rivers have the right idea, running
To their own mouths.

I want to meet an Argentine
In some casino. Have him
Ask me to come up to his place.

All the people face me, belting
The equatorial bulge.
Does the Earth want out?

You resolve to head South.
Artlessly you end up
Tongue stuck on the Arctic ice caps.

We send our prayers up. North.
It dawns on me as I revolve
I live in the East.
God is made of ice.

THE DARK SIDE OF THE MOON

We've been asked to sign up
to meet on the dark side

of the full moon. We knew
this would happen when

you mention tequila is spilling
and it never misses

when I start to say
I'm not afraid

a certified lunatic
writes *Do not say*

you have no fear.
The celestial bodies

are turning to welcome
us with banners of red

streamers they may
change my mind

I'm about to say
go alone we could live

in two different worlds
some other time but we do.

It's the lunatic moon
of the kamikaze or the perfect

binge of what is this,
this and the surprise of the other side.

A GRAPHIC MAP OF ETERNITY

If it had been a snake
or the nose on your face

we'd be excused, exhausted
looking at the dead

who've got other fish to fry.
The dead are making up

questions too hard to answer
and they still don't love each other,

so leave the dead alone.
The dead have to eat

the pearly scales of the heavenly
gates, hold up the phosphorescent

bones, to be struck by the other-
wise simple pleasure, *we didn't plan*

on our plane dropping us in
the frozen Potomac.

The dead keep the peace
and they've got things to do,

so leave the dead alone,
they'll let us know

when they want us
they'll pull out their books

they've read with a vengeance
of customs and manners.

They live in the past.
Instead let us praise the past

perfect in its repose, immovable,
exclamatory and beyond belief,

past understanding, actions,
being or states of being

perfected before some definite
past time. This is what

I would have you promise me
you've cracked gravity's lock,

your desire to give me over
and over another chance to take

what's coming to us and the air-
plane in the air are distances

that are not so much like the flip
of a coin or the flip up the steep

rise of the odds against chance,
more like what we don't understand

made flesh, steel panels that engage
and emerge routinely calculated

to do what we can't believe,
that promise to get us there,

unbruised, beyond the Milky Way,
beyond the speed of light, cruising,

all the time in the world
without a doubt we'll be struck

when we see birds flock
like metal filings against

magnetic fields, and the mercury
of moonlight rising hot and cold,

the stages the sun picks out
before us when it strikes so many ways

at once, and the names
on neon signs when they shock

a name isn't it not beyond
belief when we love

the radio because it says
picture the music

it's hard to resist it
when you offer me a ticket

that crosses the distance
which divides us you give me

no choice in this
unpredictable channel

it's scenic water,
we're in this together.

Your hand is light and everlasting,
forbidden and skin and bones

and this is called praising
by the perfection of our bodies

this is called praise
when the dead and the living

invite the unborn to drive
or be driven without destination

past a lake where under a sky
broken by jet trails and beautiful

birds a speedboat drags a laughing man
whose figure cuts a pattern

of tracks in the water
that reflects the hereafter

what I would have you promise
what is too beautiful

not to mention this
is nothing special it is

the same elsewhere not
to mention everlasting.

COLORLESS GREEN IDEAS

The color of broken stalks, they are
the wheat's sharp turn to hay.

They are the color of hospital walls;
patients sleeping, please, walk.

Will you wait, we'll try this once more.
They are some color. We keep getting closer.

They are our friends who sleep curiously
alone in their fine houses, gates latched,

surrounded by the dark which stands
like a horse in his stall, over them.

He stomps one hoof, any one of them
might wake shouting or unable to rise,

turn in waking's sad attempt to disengage
the dream's sentence, the night's quiet.

We think how difficult it is for nothing
to remain nothing. Everything resists it.

LITTLE BLACK TANGRAMS

1

No one felt in the dark for his hat.
No one budged an inch.
Thus the story draws to its end.
No one felt over the edge
of her silk pocket to touch her parking ticket.
No one even wished to
walk out of the dark into the street.

2

Over the transparent page I traced my name.
I thought about The Bird That Turns Around,
How To Blow A Brick Over, What To Do
While Waiting For The Doctor, Answers To
Problems On Page 2000, The Chair That
Comes To You, The Mysterious Paper Purse,
The Universe Around Us, *Lift To Erase.*

3

Those days everything I thought trembled
through the rotating blades of an electric fan.
The way my voice moved through it.
The way my fingers shook.
I wore a two-tiered hat.
A dead mule is huge.
The man with the stick was fat.

4

A dead deer has the face of a rat.
Last night I watched seven white deer
walk single file across the black edge,
the levee's border.
Slowly, each one looked me over,
saw I was sleeping, and soon came closer
to lick my face all over.

5

All fall I played at being a slave.
In the red embers of fires I made
I burned slips of paper with politicians' names
to pass the time.
I cooked rich soups of dragonflies.
I learned to aim an arrow
through a devilhorse's brain.

6

I sat alone by the water.
They trusted me with the river.
When United Fruit Company boats
headed for port, upriver,
I called out to sailors,
down came stalks of bananas
to snag and bring up to the batture.

7

When the polls opened until the polls closed
two men dangled their rifles over their shoulders
and pretended they couldn't be seen.
The men and women who came were embarrassed.
They looked down at the white glare
of crushed shells at their feet.
They looked off into the distance.

8

In the hot sun on the wooden platform
I stood waiting for the icehouse doors to open.
I wanted to be asked inside
the cool bricks of smoking water, frozen
and squared in fifty-pound blocks,
rattling along belts of silver rollers.
I wanted to be cool and dry.

9

The women were left locked in the house.
The rifle's blue-black barrel shone
in the corner against the white, white wall.
Somewhere in the swamps around us
a man threw himself against the dark.
I couldn't understand why our lights were on.
I wondered if he would drown.

10

I was afraid of the iridescent algae pool,
hit with glaze after an afternoon storm,
lifted like a giant keyhole,
lit by the great green eyeball behind it,
watching me, watching me turn away,
watching me look back, watching me, for all I knew,
catch my breath, not wanting to give it back.

11

We walked into the parking lot
after ten o'clock mass on Sunday.
A car's blur crossed our path
so close I felt the heat of the sun
in the hot wind off its fender.
They only meant to scare us.
I felt then what my prayers might have been.

12

That afternoon someone decided to slaughter the rabbits.
They held the scruffs of their necks,
whacked their soft brown crowns
with cracked baseball bats.
Each one bled through the nose.
We fed their guts to the alligator
by the shed in the deep, deep hole.

13

I watched them kissing, kissing in sorrow,
in the sitting rooms in the funeral parlor.
They were drinking café au lait
and eating ham sandwiches.
Yes, there were so many flowers.
I didn't want to be kissed in sorrow.
I didn't want to be patted or pitied.

14

The squeak and thump and mist of flit
as someone pumped sprays of insecticide.
It fell over my face, like a blessing,
like a tingling sensation in my fingers,
like a thousand evaporating lessons,
it fell on the oil lamp's wick.
The flame danced. It wobbled, dipped and brightened.

DAYTRIP TO PARADOX

Just as you'd expect
my preparations were painstaking
            and exact. I took two

butane lighters and a cooler
            of ice. I knew the route
            had been so well traveled

            there'd be a store for necessities
and tobacco and liquor and axes.
            And near the Utopian village of Nucla

            three golden eagles watched me
from a salt cedar tree. One of them
            held its third talon hard in the eye

of a white northern hare. Audubon
            couldn't have pictured it better.
                        Everything was perfect. Naturally

            it made me think of Siberia,
the bright inspirational star
            that's handed down the generations,

and the long, terrible nights
            of the pioneers' journey to paradise.
            The valley on the way to Paradox

            was flat, there would be no choice,
nothing to get me lost.
            Cattle guards, gates, and fencing

bordered the open range. Of course
    I crossed a narrow bridge
        to get into Paradox proper.

    In the store that doubled
as town hall and post office
        there was an account book for everybody

laid square on the counter.
    No one was expected to pay
        hard cold cash in Paradox apparently.

STILL IN WONDER

The children went out into their world,
a ragged field they'd already explored,
already fought off other children for,
and found, as if left to them alone,
a sharp-eared, long-haired pony
looking at them with longing.
They'd wished for mornings like this,
their fathers and mothers gone,
the green grass wet, the sun not strong
enough to hurt, the perfect gift,
left without a catch, not so much
as distant relatives to thank.
Their horse. Theirs. Eidetic.
What they didn't know they'd asked
to have, here, now and no one
saying get, get, go on home, it's mine.
And tame. As they approached,
their eyes and the eyes of the horse
wound toward one another like lovers.
Their hands found their places
over the horse's mane, fetlock, small back
and haunch, their mouths still in wonder
until one of them wanted to ride,
and then another, and then them all
until one of them found the courage
to climb on. All morning they rode
over the trampled grass, they thought
of nothing else, they couldn't get enough.
When the horse began to tire, stumble,
falter and fall, they kicked it on,
pulled it farther by its cheeks

and backwards by its tail,
they picked up sticks to beat it back to life,
they went so far they never could return,
they lied to one another about how to make it work.

HYPNAGOGIC

It began with the egg-and-dart,
sunrise, animal, diamond work, palmette,

running ornament, tumbled brick, the fret.
Nothing for me to do but shut my eyes

and wait and they'd arrive. Cornices,
shafts and capital pediments, entablature,

gambrel gables, dentils and brackets.
I learned fast the part I had to take.

Not to make a move, not to edge my sight beyond.
They'd come around alone or not at all.

And they'd dissolved, one into the other
or they'd be gone. Not for me to invite

or rearrange or they'd shut down.
And when they upped the ante I obeyed:

in flayed hideous faces, in plain white skulls
without eyes, in griffins, in malevolent freaks,

in living dead chimeras. So I could not move,
fascinated, then afraid I'd have them with me

all my life to carry on. But they didn't stop
at that. They gave me the faces of strangers:

receptionist staring at the thermostat
as she takes my name, car wash money changer,

postal clerk ringing my receipt, ID checker,
customs officer, bank teller, airport security

guard, poll watcher, doorman, elevator operator,
bouncer. In remote silence I watched serial strangers.

In spite of my will to intervene I complied.
In the lull before sleep I waited for them,

lonely, adrift, and nearly lost, restless,
about as good as dead if they didn't appear.

They were training me to wait and not want
what I'd lose if I asked for it.

I had to pretend I didn't care
and this was against my nature.

LIFE BASED ON A WORTHLESS DARE

That's one god-awful way
to set foot in this world.

What kinds of sorry particulars
and principles I'd have

to be stuck with there.
Knowing this about myself

all my life.
I'd be ashamed.

That makes it hard.
It makes me faceted

like the eyes of a fly.
Pretty in tiny isolation

and idly misprized.
About as bad as having believed

I'd thrown it all about as far
away as I could get it

and lo and behold not only had I
not but also I'd been wrong.

Guilt's got it all over us.
Guilt's an original sin

like regret built into pleasure,
like the so-called natural world.

Was it like now then for Niels Bohr,
or Kierkegaard or Rutherford, Hahn,
or William James, or Bellamy or H.G. Wells?

Today's Wells's birthday
and I'm having a party without him.
I've invited a man with a mission

and a woman without a will.
Just now a bee's flown up my dress
and dug deeply down into my tender flesh.

That's how it goes. Up in the air
it's the triumph of trompe l'oeil,
there's music, neutrinos, and microwaves,

it's the world of the modernaire.
I went there with a Chicago broker
and his unbroken wife to their third house

in the country atop a vacant mesa,
a string of vintage trailers
and amusing paraphernalia, nickel Coke

signboards, raggedy bobcats and antique
rattan wheelchairs, scavenged contraptions.
They'd accidentally named it Rancho Deluxe.

At the moment that's no more than memory.
The broker was making some possible arrangements
to sacrifice his life for the sake of humanity

as well as material wealth. I was, by then, reclined
more or less on an extraordinarily expensive rug.
I was big, I was huge. Bigger than monumental

buildings, bigger than transcontinental trains,
bigger than barnyards of docile, fattened animals.
I was that way for years. I was big, I tell you.

I was huge. I carried the world around in a sack,
pieced it together, tore it down and fixed it back.
There wasn't one single thing I lacked.

Before that I was something else altogether.
No doubt I was one thing to my mother.
To my father, something else again.

I was the sweet smell of sex between the sheets,
then an earth-grinding spiral of DNA molecules.
It'd be sweet to think I was an angel.

A HANDFUL OF PORCUPINE QUILLS

I confess I threw away what
I should have kept.

Something happened upon
at a wrong turn

in my unsteady step.
I knew when I threw it in

with scraps and swill
and spoils and glistening innards

I'd be sorry later.
And I am.

For the briefest moment
I haggled it in my hand,

I saw its every important angle,
its translucent, lasting beauty,

its long, honorable history.
I knew I would be glad

to keep it with me.
It might have attached my wrist

to a bright thread of light
and led me right on up

into the web of the pattern
of the manifest world

that didn't change.
But I threw it in.

LONGING

I'd like your bony hand
going through my hair;

I'd like it touching
the contours of my skull.

That would make me calm.
I wouldn't have anything more

to say but maybe I'd hum
like an arroyo of bees.

It isn't easy is it?
Longing is something you do

alone, addressing everything
that's been or will be.

How could you hope
to feel at peace? See how

despair comes next, part
of longing's own ecology,

hungry egrets pecking insects
off the necks of grazing bulls.

I notice how often a smile
is an apology, how an apology

is full of self-regard by necessity.
It is so cold in my room.

You know how it feels
to believe nothing else matters,

something thinks through you
with a mind of its own.

It makes us seem small together
being each one what we are alone

when we long as one.
It's probably a sin

to make an idol of it.
I have sometimes done so.

WINSLOW HOMER'S BLUES

Though the book was not meant
for me, it's hard to resist

a man's good art,
like resisting a sweet

and secret kiss, stolen
from or meant for another.

I picked up the book
and looked at it cover to cover.

It's that way with books,
they have no single owner.

Crossing the pages, my eyes
stopped to linger

over the sheer depths
of a dimensionless dark water,

surfaces I haven't anticipated,
fish, frog, lily, moth, exact,

particular, penetrating eyes
which looked right back,

two silver-black marks
I might take for a mosquito hawk,

plain red sun going down
over the anonymous horizon

like a cynic's Icarus.
He stood his apple pickers

at ease where golden air
fell through the meshes

of the leaves of shadows,
blackboard lessons in circles,

parallel lines and holy triangles,
and the deeper, fourth dimension,

lightened by a schoolmarm's apron,
checkered, her left arm thrown

behind her straight back, to hold
her right arm's elbow up.

He made his bodies as if someone
he loved would be living in them,

or someone living would like to be
near them to lean upon.

He showed how humans stand
and wait with their honest day's

work in their hands
for the ones they love to return

when where they've been
has been far off and treacherous.

He invited me in with candor,
humor, care, and skill

into what invited him.
In love, longing, or despair,

I've never walked his pliant beaches,
I've gone and walked elsewhere.

Though I would gladly have
been with him. His blues

matched mine in two ways.
He loved his blues

in likely and unlikely places
and made generous sense

of a composition's shape
by where he put them.

He made apples blue
and plums, canoes, and shoes

on reclining girls. He picked
blues for shutters and blues

for skirts and for Parliament,
blues for shirts and sails,

blues for fish, blue for the plough,
blues in waters and in clouds,

blues in eyes and for blue sky,
rising and falling, blues

for fresh air. I was grateful
to lose myself in Homer's blues.

I closed the book and put it back
with its blue spine unbroken.

TWO

THE WHITE BOAT

The birds are sleeping, it's far from morning,
except for the birds who rightfully haunt
the dark, and the low-life, lazy geese
who've given up their flyway rights
to live at ease around the man-made pond
below the ridge. They come around the hour
of the wolf and wake me up. I can't help but
love their haunting, honking grief.
It sounds like grief tonight.
A white boat in full moon light is rocking
on the lawn. It rocks and rocks
like a giant's cradle or a mammoth's bassinet.
It rocks like a cradle for a god or a devil.
The white boat doesn't want to go home.

APOLOGY FOR AND FURTHER EXPLANATION OF AN ATTEMPT TO DIVERT ACCUSATIONS OF EQUIVOCATION

In my hometown it was like January,
like January in Oaxaca, in Fortin

de las Flores, like Fortin
in the midforties, like the '40s

in December, like December
on the river, a forest of willows

half in, half out of water,
like the river in the picture,

like the picture above your bureau,
like your bureau filled to overflowing

with feathers every color of the spectrum,
feather blown through vowels,

through curtains of bougainvillea, going
on forever, forever as it formerly was,

in the luster of a loved one's luggage,
baggage to carry lightly or solemnly

toss off into the Bay of Fundy.
Thank you for four golden mice

who never wake me up at night,
for the pocket-size surveillance device,

for books which tell me nothing's unakin.
In January it was like my hometown

in the 1940s in the middle of December,
December a cool glass of water at noon

in the summer, a clinking of cowbells
to signal it's evening. I was seven,

four, eight, eleven, still unborn,
brother to my younger sister,

sister to my mother, father like a twin,
twins like vapor trails on clear nights

in October. You were my shadow
I dared not step into. You stood by

my shoulder, champion, angel, faithful
companion I dared not look in the eye.

What was it like for you?
Were you about to step into your skin,

like water poured from a pitcher,
like an ant into amber, like molten gold?

Was the gold like someone's fortune
or folly, folly a moving picture you'd get

into for a quarter, when a quarter meant
more than a dollar, a dollar a bit

of a future you'd be expected to furnish,
I'd be with you to finish,

of a finish wearing the date of your birth,
polished with everyone's hopes,

polished with everyone's dreams,
lost in a basket of keepsakes.

5½ INCH LULLABY

When something he would never know,
when something happened to him,
when he was too young to remember,
when it reminded him,
when he knew all along,
when someone lies about something,
when it doesn't mean it isn't true,
when he was too young to remember,
when he was sleepy and friendly with thoughts,
when he'd spent the day gathering,
when his head touched his pillow,
when he was too young to remember,
when it stood among his towns, runways, train
      routes, and farms,
when each animal had a name, a place,
      and a purpose,
when it remained as he made it,
when he wanted to change it,
when something confused and cluttered
      everything he'd spent the day building,
when his jetfighters sank in his rivers,
when his frogs on their lily pads floated
      to the tops of his tilting skyscrapers,
when he was finally falling asleep,
when his room floated above the other rooms,
when noises and music and voices rose,
when the legionnaire stays true to his dream,
when another goes on and on,
when a tone without words takes on form,
when the wonders of everything wear down,
someone steps into the room.

INTERVIEW

What was it you first noticed?
I found her stupefied, in the oven,
dumbfounded, stunned, in her oven.
And then? Then I found her again,
tasting a shoe she'd baked.
How did you feel? I had no words
for that. I hadn't felt
anything approaching it.
Can you describe anything else?
Can you say anything more about,
about how you felt when you knew?
I didn't know.
Can you say something more, something
about the way you felt about it?
It continually interrupted me,
anything I might have felt.
I was absorbed.
Then what, what happened next?
She began licking her hands, no, first
it was her eyes, she'd touch them.
And then? Then what was left?
I don't know. I wanted to lend her
something, though whatever that
might have been is lost to me.
Did you keep track of her activities?
No, yes, well, they were eradicating.
Well, let's go back
to specifics. Can you say
anything about her habits?
She'd lost that thought. She had none.
She had none? She floated? Uh-huh,

every day there were plans to consider.
Plans? Yes. What sort of plans?
A nail had come loose from a vortex
she'd driven. The tread on the tires
wore away. Something about filters.
It was an idea under siege.
Under siege? Embattled. You understand,
nothing I wanted to say could help.

FLY ON THE WALL

Back in the '30s he'd done his bit,
making big money in the sci-fi camp,
squirreling it away in real estate scams
and rare books.
I'd flown in for his annual solstice party
to watch him do his party trick.
He'd rigged his party lights to flick on and off
with just the touch of his fingertip
on a snake plant's stalk.
I could walk all night long over the same surface
with absolutely zero effect.
His guest list was never long,
enormous twins in sea green satin gowns
with phosphorescent tiaras on,
a string bean of a man in a skintight suit,
lugging around a nose-making kit,
a troop of Brownies with stethoscopes,
killing jars, relaxing changers and insect pins.
I was feeling queasy and my heart beat poorly.
But the old commander always sensed
my unnerved concern and invited me down
into his rare book room.
He showed me the broken spines of books he loved
and books he'd never sell. He told me stories
about men and women who jerked books around,
who shouted and screamed at books,
who breathed on them.
He whispered to me tales of books
he'd seen lying in gutters
and books used for doorstops and paperweights.
He showed me a book wrapped in cellophane,

its pages uncut, its binding sharp as his eyes,
and said it had been the murder weapon
in an ancient assassination.
He told me about my cousins who eat books,
glue, paper, and ink, and stand on the library's steps
and brag and give speeches about it.
He did not seem surprised
that I should have never known
how many bugs live in books all their lives.
He pointed to a book in which it is written
how one pair of flies, left to their own desires,
will produce 25 generations of offspring
in fewer than 365 days. Our numbers, if left unchecked,
could increase to fill a ball 96 million miles wide.
My kind of flies!
Flies, he breathed, with no time for books.
He went on telling me how most people treat books
like bricks, how most books stand lonely and unread
on dirty shelves, cities for spiders,
ballast for drifters, seasonal gifts,
touched barely once and forgotten.
He brought out books faded by the light of day
and books strong as giants
that broke other books down,
that bullied other books into submission,
and a few that stood firm in any circumstance
protecting weak and sick books
that could not defend themselves.
He pulled down *The Insect World of Henri Fabre*
and let me crawl over its tender insinuations.
A crisp, uncirculated twenty-dollar bill

fell to the floor from page 20.
We stared at it, my old friend and I,
the way galaxies gaze upon history.
I hauled myself into the safety of the depths
of his trousers' rolled cuff
and we crept up the steps to ride out
the rest of the party. The ladies in green
crooned old lullabies to the Brownies.
Every nose in the galley was set right on its face.
I clung to the wall and thought of the stranger
who'd wielded a book to flatten my mother.
While the cold evening turned into morning
the old commander palpated his party lights
and cranked up his old Victrola.
I flew to his side and stood like a dog
by his master. We listened to secrets
that pass between strangers
who've spent the evening eyeing each other.
A loaded sailor in earmuffs strolled near
and looked me over. Hey, flyweight, he muttered,
who do you think you are?
Who me, I faltered, me, I'm nobody,
I'm the half deaf fly on the wall.
The commander fluffed my bristles, tapped
my orbital plate, and adjusted my crooked antennae.
He shooed me toward the transom
out of the way of my incessant fate.
Tomorrow would last a few minutes longer.

DON'T SAY MY NAME

Skull, axis, kernel of focus,
hub of center, genius of crisis,

brain, swaddled in silken tufts,
shawl, veil, scarf, majestic loft.

Listing, harebrained, keeling,
right side up and upside down,

one big lonesome brain searching
through eternity for eyes, arms, legs,

forty acres and a mule,
kind neighbors, good luck, faithful

lovers. Big, guileless baby of a brain
searching through eternity

with cracks in its skull
nerve endings escape,

attracting bees like honey,
lightning bolts like thoughts,

nerve endings like smoky moths.
What fool thinks of strands

of hair as passing thoughts?
Who wants to comb them all

morning and stroke them back
to sleep all night?

Whose hands haven't
felt as if they've detached

to careen through space
like stray thoughts of a lost planet,

searching through space for your hair,
to touch it, to worship its source?

UNTITLED

It gives us a chance to lean close to a friend,
to brush the simple crumb of chocolate

from his shirt before it melts.
Or it lets us touch a bead of sleep

a lover's eye protects.
It makes it possible to make a wish,

to see an eyelash prevent a car crash,
or keep what we love from harm's way.

It protects us as well from those creeps
who think of us as legal tender

in their private stock of fodder.
Oh, it can turn up as a fly in good soup, but

it was put there on purpose, by the cook.
It spins all of the everywhere unraveling

loose threads straight back to their spindle,
back through music, through time and space

and television and breakfast cereal, through
petroleum and photosynthesis each in its season.

It distributes chromosomes as if chromosomes
counted for something. And it costs us nothing.

It's as easily overlooked as Mars lights
or pistol grips. It's nothing like anything

you'd find in a footnote. Whoever even thinks
to steal it spontaneously combusts and leaves

all evidence and memory without a trace.
Whoever claims to name it loses his name,

and the names of his ancestors and children
go up in smoke. It disturbs only those

for whom value equals the sum of cost, who
disturb sleeping dog, on whom everything is lost.

It distributes itself regardless of age, class,
race, club affiliation or sex, food groups, genius,

or reason. It can be found on page 29
of the book you're always telling someone to read.

Over all inquisitions, crusades, haircuts, contracts,
and baptisms it witnesses. Ambulance chasers

and pornographers get their share right along
with the bystanders. It does not interfere

with anyone's career. It's there for the wars
and for the breaking of treaties, when half

the world's sleeping and the other half weeps.
It's up on the shelf in the back of the closet,

down in the cellar, down in the Titanic.
It drew you as close as you've ever come

to what you must fear. It's on the cuffs of technicians
when they fiddle with switches.

It stands by the executioner when he decides
what to wear.

A SECRET LIFE

The not-quite-invisible flowers
on the farthest edges

of out-of-the-way meadows
should not speak of it.

And yet they listen.
Their spans of silent attention

embarrass ardent lovers.
Cats intent on unreachable sparrows

look dementedly distracted
compared to these faithful flowers.

Imaginary walls go down,
walls of reinforced steel rise up,

walls of paper, plaster, walls
of ice, walls of brick, straw,

mud, gingerbread, and glass.
The light-sensitive, photo-optic,

technologically advanced wall of louvers
has a mind of its own.

It's useless to hope
to break its concentration.

When I returned I found four walls
surrounded by a new idea, a bakery.

I pretended to be hungry
for their bread and cakes

so I could go inside.
So many years had passed

the bakers didn't know me
or that my life had gone by inside

the rooms their fragrant ovens filled.
I imagined myself once again

entering the lives of saints and animals
who never failed to welcome me,

a long-lost sister, a stranger.
Our tenderness toward one another

never, never faltered.
My thoughts have hidden themselves

from everything available
which might have made them visible.

An evergreen hedge may take
half a woman's life to grow

and then what should she put inside—
a few plain, domestic anachronisms—

woodpiles, abandoned cars, clotheslines,
a necessary lie, a grave you should

have taken to the grave?
My terminally-ill neighbor hid

herself from me with rows of arborvitae.
I told myself she cared for me

enough to protect me from her misery.
Was that another lie?

Nothing can protect me
from what churns up inside.

My illness secreted itself
where none could bring themselves

to find it. So much of what we do
in secret we don't know we do.

We dream of what we really are
and spend lifetimes denying it.

That was just a dream
I say, forgetting it.

Dreams don't come true,
says the empty bucket,

sloshing with imaginary water,
as it's hauled up by the hand

of a nonexistent stranger
hoping to quench my infinite thirst.

Near the end of his life
Henry Adams spent an evening

telling his young niece all he knew
because she would not understand

a word of it and so would never
quote him. Poor Henry.

I REMEMBER RILKE

I remember Rilke sopping wet,
sprawled out as usual
all over his lilac bed,
newfangled breezes firing up
his freezing rooms,
crumbs of sesame drugs
loose in his killer hair.
Like 91% of the rest of us
he lied about the time
he spent alone.
He spent most of his time
on the telephone.
And the rest in pursuit
of a spider he'd run across
at supper, striding up
his butter knife.
He was one handsome devil,
all tensile muscle
built for rapid travel.
He never once said please
or hesitated to crawl
into dinner plates.
Such a relief to see
a grown, living spider,
astride a trivet, declaiming
against minutiae by simple
virtue of his bearing,
the unrequired champion
of infinity, enjoying himself
at the table, encouraging
Rilke to commit to memory

his adoration of a certain
shade of violet. Without
apology, without so much as
a nod toward regret, he ambled
up a woman's arm and turned
like a friendly bracelet around
her sensible wrist. I don't
remember truly much more about Rilke.

AFTER THE BIRDS LEARNED TO COUNT TO EIGHT

In any case everyone felt obligated
to have an opinion or at least an opinion
regarding your opinion if you had one.
Often enough passing thoughts evolved
into convictions. Some were etched in stone,
some decided to go it alone, many were suspended,
many stood up like feathers in our caps.
We were distant and we were near North America's
geographic center. It was never where
we thought it was. Our skullcaps, our secret
lubrications fooled the sun we bet on, the sun
we agreed stayed up there. All the old codgers
burrowed in nearby and held up hand-lettered
signs: NO SIGNS OF LIFE FOUND HERE.
We took that to mean do something useful,
say sign up for four-hand piano at least,
or something along those lines, requiring the use
of all of our fingers and most of our time.
We would also need a gazebo, an array of vendors
(corn dogs, frozen bananas, fried frog, quail grog),
Hmong quilters, greenpeacers, sandal zealots,
a chamber of commerce, additional security, and
fire personnel. We were to remain extemporaneous,
at all cost. But cost wasn't a factor, money
didn't matter! When we protested we had no talent
our music teachers protested back. Our teachers
lacked the requisite attacks of conscience.
They wanted to convince us we could be good.
They'd harmonize good's as good as a plain doorknob,
as they clunked our heads together to smart us
into devotional attitudes. So, all right, we'd perform

what we couldn't learn. Such stern teachers we had,
with soft hearts, too, so it got to be our job
to convince them they'd tried as hard as they could.
Straight A's for them. To their dismay, to their
apoplexy. Anyway, the midwives were mixing it up
with the morticians over punch bowls of galactic
proportions. One of the planets in our solar system
might be blown out of the water tomorrow.
And we thought it was our millennium.
We would all wear handsomely tailored life jackets
and cheer one another on with old camp songs.
Everyone would eat recently vintaged peas,
an industrial accident everybody praised.
The children just followed along, caught
in our wake, bobbing up and down like corks
in a great salt lake.

COMPANY

Then there came the day my friends
did everything they did
at the same time together.
They looked exactly like one another.
I said it made me mad.
I meant it had me all confused.
Clothes, hats, cars, shoes, books, food,
all the same. I no longer knew who
might be who and received a good deal
of sympathy. They had me so confused.
Now I can barely arrange myself properly
for company. Most recently two of my friends
celebrated the day Coca-Cola was invented.
That's a success story. All day they'd been
wanting hamburgers. Between friends
nothing is forbidden. They like mayonnaise,
lettuce, tomatoes, onions, on toast,
with roasted chiles and cheese.
The conversation revolved around horses.
About taking care of horses on their way
to slaughterhouses, about what a market
there is for horse in France, of course,
but also in Scandinavian countries where
they like their horse in sausage along with
eels in aspic. There's a discrete market
for horse in America, which turns out to be
a forbidden topic. I didn't know veal
happens to be less prized in France than beef,
or that there is not now nor has there ever
been anything there we could call a ranch.
I loved all my friends even as they persisted

in tricking me, which amounted to telling me
the truth about everything all at once.
Pulses of weather disturbances encouraged me.
The sun shone on spring leaves, then it
hailed and the temperature dropped forty degrees.
Down to the minute, down to the man, everyone
agreed we must uncomplicate our lives.

OUR MASTER PLAN

Celeste goes waltzing with bears.
Natalie shops for milk glass on pedestals
modeled after the hooves of baby goats.
Mr. Holdrogen whips in and out of his tuxedo
faster than a pileated woodpecker
can count without a calculator.
Mark and Peg corner the market on legible parakeets.
Spencer's attention to our master plan strays.
Pam invents a netherworldly new perfume.
We rule out Aperçu.
David monikers it Template.
Peter knows the time has come to run as fast as he can.
Jean Marie finally adopts a highway,
mind-boggling the numbers of chipmunks and squirrels
who survive her drive-by cleaning services.
Emily discovers a secret room adjoins the room
of her own.
Spencer stays out of trouble attaching animals
to their woodland shadows, thereby contemplating
the stuff of the origins of good and evil.
Master Hauggins completes his masterpiece,
Persons of Apparently Little or No Peerage,
yet remains self-abnegating, protesting gently
we oughtn't have named our plan after him.
A.J. and Grace move to Rome.
Valerie and John come home.
Guy reenacts for Bjorn a battle he witnessed
between Bennington, Vermont and Amherst, Massachusetts.
Spencer receives orders to count epiphanies.
Mr. You-Know-Who presents Spencer a handheld,

stainless steel tally meter to make the job easier.
Spencer appears more confused than ever,
more confused than a beaver
in a waterfall in a shopping mall.
We rule out shopping malls.
Teresa swears off kielbasa, swears by Gertrude Stein.
Alyce teaches the first lady the trick
of a feminized sucker punch.
Deveraux loses his keys in a 40-acre maze of corn.
Jerry grows little goatees in both of his ears.
Dave Marley and Stephen hitchhike among the great
sequoias.
Yesho takes London to Turkey to meet the family.
Master Hauggins announces his next topic,
What to Do for Your Friends Marginalized by Fame.
Stuart and Mary spend a splendid evening swimming
in New York City's most glamorous swimming hole.
Claudia and Vernon visit St. Augustine.
Monica and Monique grow up.
Ycola finds it in her heart to forgive her mother
and her father and all of the rest of us.
Uncle Stack lays down his sister-in-law's
wedding bouquet on his brother's grave
and sits down beside them and cries.
Spencer returns Mr. You-Know-Who's tally meter.
It does not bring out the best in either.
Johnny Konik marries too quickly
after his wife suddenly dies.
Lydia fools herself into thinking she can impress
anyone by eating crabs with a knife and fork.

Claire no longer holds it against her long-lost
goddaughter.
Uncle Dude's thirteen kids divide up his land
amongst themselves and stay put.
Aunt Pom's death appears and disappears
like an air mint in her sister's mouth.
Gerard never misses a day without someone
to give him a shave.
Euphrasie spends all afternoon on the porch
untangling her niece's hair.
Cid spots a pair of geese he'll come back
at dusk to shoot.
Marguerite's mind goes up in smoke.
Sister Stephanie is Sister Edward's lover.
Bishop Aloysius excommunicates the racist.
Uncle Richie shakes JFK's hand on Halloween.
And so on and so on, so goes our master plan.

ALL IN A DAY'S WORK

Even our children had things to say
about the death penalty,

about executing authority,
about how close to reality they came

to punching out one another's lights.
I couldn't help but hold back a tear

when our son said he loved street banners
no matter how they read.

"To dig a hole in the middle of City Park,
to burn yourself up, is it legal?"

It's your life, our daughter remarks,
you can take it any way you want.

All's clear just about then.
Mrs. Frog's all settled in the Inn.

As we recall, Mr. Frog's gone around the bend.
Everyone was in a big rush

to join the soccer casualties of America.
Nobody was listening to anybody.

We looked at one another meaningfully.

The carnivores had located their suppers.
The herbivores gazed across the empty range.

THE SOUP DRILL

The time it takes certain fashions to change,
say, togas to pantaloons, wigs to pierced nipples,
correlates inversely to the time it takes to bore
a handful of holes into an ice cube of pesto.
Some ideas last about as long as it takes frozen
soup to defrost. Cowpokes like to yodel on about
how much easier it is to break an unbroken colt.
Fact is, going on the last fifty years, rustlers
mostly work out of helicopters.
Time was, every other rustler's mother committed
to memory her old family remedies.
Who do I think put the stars up there?
What do I think the ladle is for?

WITHOUT A SIMILAR CONDITION INCLUDING
THIS CONDITION

The farther away from the center of power
you build your house

the longer your lightbulbs will last.
An electrician told me.

Through fog, through buds
and leaves touched with red

before they turn colors,
I ponder the blind horse

as it follows the flanks of its mate
through the pasture.

The horse with good eyes
grazes.

I've never seen it run.
The blind horse keeps its head

never more than a few feet away
from its friend.

IF I WERE A RAPTOR CRUISING THROUGH
THE TIMETABLES OF HISTORY

I would want you to come with me into those years
in which it is recorded that nothing happened in
Daily Life, so maybe we could stir something up.
We could listen for the syllables in a famous Arab's
epic and watch tea appear in China.
Maybe we could warn the alchemists to take better care
of their products.
Like drop-ins to a séance we might enter those eras
in which it is recorded nothing happened in Music.
And say this is impossible.
And since it appears not a year's gone by without
something happening in politics, maybe you could run
for office and refuse election, maybe we could throw
out enough monkey wrenches so as to effect some different
outcomes.
Longer ago than 3,000 years no one had imagined
labor strikes in Thebes.
There was no Hebrew alphabet.
No trumpet-playing competitions anywhere at all.
Nobody had seen a catapult.
And we'd have to pack our own lunch
because there were no chickens in Babylon.

IS IT YOU?

Whose clouds are those? Whose nematodes?
Whose clover?
What enters your mind when you put on your coat?
There's a story I'm longing to whisper in your ear.
Isn't it a story we've already heard?
Will you stop and be with me awhile over the dewpoint?
Will you touch me?
Is it you who brings terror to lonely places?
Did you take the snapshot of the second before the Last
Judgment, the moment when the lids have lifted from all
of the coffins but the dead haven't noticed it yet?
Did you coin the expression, *sleep with the angels?*
Did you know how the living would fight over the dearly departed?
Why did you hide consolation in a crack in the trunk
of an olive tree on an island hardly anyone gets to anymore?
Was it you who tanned me in sumac and bound me to a book?
Did you blind the cat so the mouse could return to its nest?
Is it you I can't hold enough of in my galvanized hands?
Did you direct sunlight to shape a grazing horse's neck
so that no one can look at it and not say they ache?
Did you understand how difficult it would be to think
of hair growing or birds in flight or a moon turning?
Did you turn a bushel upside down in a corner so that
light could hide in it?
Is it you who treated air as if it were a broth
fragrant with alleys of bay leaves and so clear you saw
your own face in it?
Is it you holding the keys for the locks on the doors
to the beautiful empty room?

ONE ENCHANTED EVENING

You found me in quicksand
and did not ask me stupid questions.
You peeled a mandarin drake
and did not ask me to watch.
You sent away the doctors
and the doctors of the church.
You photographed an indigo mosquito hawk
and showed me the result.
You crosshatched something in a book
and lowered the brim of your hat.
You touched a long pole to the top of my head
and walked in circles around me.
You kept the measure of the distance between us
inside a secret pocket.
You pried open an oyster
and kept your eyes shut.
You poured yourself a glass of cold vodka
and did not offer me any.
You picked up a dispatch in a bottle
and did not ask me to witness it.
You brought me a lop-eared rabbit
and let me watch it sleep.
You showed me a cicada still in its tuxedo
and let me watch it eat an elder leaf.
Seasons came and seasons went
and in between a boy and girl grew up.
You did not ask me what that was about.
You sang awhile to the stars and the wind
and did not let me stop you.

A CAGED-IN EXPOSITION OF CONCEPTIONS EVOLVED IN LOGIC AND WORDS: A LOVE STORY

An entire afternoon without speaking.
Vow of silence.
A bumblebee flew out of the hibiscus.
Did you see the boy fly out of the man?
Everyone has a different name for the color of the sky.
Someone said, "Can you lend me a little fuel
for my analogy machine?"
We ask the children to memorize in many different
languages the sentence that says: Our parents
are deaf and dumb but we have not had unhappy
childhoods.
For oh so long in Paris, German cartographers
transposed Italian into Latin.
My thoughts fly about like a hand in the dark
in an unfamiliar house.
Or a horse in a burning stable.
Or a waterhose under too much pressure.
Or a cobra in a trance scaling the bars of heatwaves.
I love him because he knows you can't stop a ghost
with a cork.
I love him all afternoon as he unbends the bent-over
blades of grass we slept on all morning.
I love him through the evening as he untangles
and tangles my hair.

THIEF OF SPARKS

God was coming from an unnamed galaxy
with a can opener and an attitude
and stargazer lilies and tassels.
Inflorescence comes to town on Mondays,
if I remember correctly. In early June
a doe tastes grapes in half-baked fields
at around five in the morning.
And long after our glaciers have excused themselves
a prehistoric lizard's alarm goes off
and it shrugs its shoulders and lifts its head
into warm January fog. If I remember correctly,
you found me hiding beneath a bed reading a book
about tickling and kissing. You offered me a Seckel pear.
I wanted to return the sugar, eggs, vanilla, and
the broken fence. If I remember correctly,
you were two generals exchanging prisoners
in meadowsoups of sulfur.
If I remember correctly, your face was lit
with the strike of a match and the glow of a pot
of electrified tulips, all white.
My eyes rolled back into their containers,
their pain clinics, they could not longer look
at a snow leopard patrolling an onyx maze in moonlight.

ON THE OWNERSHIP OF TIME

Might as well be the ownership of time
as of anything else—you, me, them, us all
on friendly, handshaking terms, no doubt,
getting bolted upright by lightning thoughts
of bright, very bright futures, smoothing
that down with fuzzy handprints, our satinet
spreadsheets—Stop there.
"Nostalgia over one's own demise requires
thickly padded, nonporous gloves to be worn
at all times. Only then does one dare
to smooth down the hairs of time which frightened
by your very presence, your thick desire,
stand stock-still upright, frozen in fear
of you, of course."
I can't pretend to guess if I'll get anywhere
by going through all this.
"Last night you explained to me lightning
is a shadow, an aftershock, and it's shooting up
into the sky not the other way around.
The film footage you illustrated this by means of
was extraordinary and I could not sleep
I'd been so convinced and so wrong for very long."
Sometimes someone close to me will whisper
things like this to someone near my side,
someone who hides behind the mask of time or
a screen door in broad daylight or a lightfall
like the blindlight briefly felt when a bulb explodes.
Torches. "Don't we say we're buying a little
time?" Oh how I wish someone would say a little more
so I could understand what it is we're paying with.
I ask my friends about it when we're milling around on

the porch, taking down to eat slice by slice
a jicama minaret we've built and doused with lime.
We're clinking our ice, just killing time.
Such bravado in the flash a match lights
the shifting mood to mood. "All you need are two
industrial-size stainless steel salad bowls,
a foot or two of drainpipe and a solid base
to stand it on; you can monitor the entire world's
temperature." Sometimes someone whose head is in my lap
will look up and say,
"Will this happen before I'm gone?"
This might be the exploration of Mars, the cure
for an incurable disease, or the melting of all
the ice in the world.

A PEEP OF SAINTS

Saints on wallpaper, in carts and minivans,
saints on carpets, in intervals, crawl spaces
teeming with saints, a tidy sum of them massing
on the flagpoles. I once saw a saint sink
into a hammock and another saint sit on a hassock
and one fall asleep on an ottoman.
I saw a saint smiling at me.
Their smiles are so enigmatic, no teeth showing,
no spittle, no sputtering, almost nothing.
I thought I heard a saint in a surrey clomping
through the nightvistas, chewing on something.
A saint on a beeline.
A saint with a bell on.
I saw a saint walk halfway across a room
using all ten saintly toes at a time.
I couldn't complete that saint's thought.
I heard a saint bark.
I saw a saint's footprints in a cornfield
and followed them.
I found a saint on a string,
sleeping by the foot of a singing boy.
Four saints entertained me with their arias.
I saw a small saint chase a large saint for the fun of it.
I saw a saint smoke a cigarette and one paint a go-cart.
I listened to a saint beat on a soup pot.
A picture of a saint walking with a tiger
on a city street nearly stopped my heart.
I bought a needlepoint bookmark in a saint's shop.
A saint wrote my name on a grain of rice and fed
it to a titmouse.
A saint with good coordination, with patience, a saint

with a mission, with a good curveball.
A saint called me on the phone so that saintly voice
could soothe my ragged brain waves.
A saint offered me good advice.
I watched a saint open a book and stare off into space.
A saint surrounded me and sorted my dreams from my
nightmares.
I saw a saint unbutton a shirt.
I felt a saint's breath flow into my ear.
I saw a saint stand on a branch and bounce into thin air.

HIDDEN ASSETS

The collapsed barn
down on Cemetery Road

has been burned down.
I love how you call it

desuetude.
Crumbling slates slake off

the broken-down rooftop
over the bedroom

where through its window
there by the bedside,

a glass of milk,
an open storybook.

Really right after the eerie buzz of abstract thinking,
not mine, though in mine, as if an obsessed sound
technician spent a lifetime condensing the invisible
noises mayflies' wings make, and implanting the chip
of this monument to imagination gone just slightly
awry in my flight path on the way to my footpath on
the way to my car just after I left the car museum
no sooner did I wish to be back at the beginning of
seeing it for the first time, just like when we got back
from our latest trip no sooner had we unpacked
did I wish we were not even there yet. Upon leaving
the car museum one must pass through a turnstile
which I gather is there so at the day's end an attendant
can count the number of us who left to compare with
the number of us who paid a little to get in. I, for
one, would have liked to be alone in the museum but
I could not be trusted not to touch, not to touch so
much begging to be touched, petted, stroked,
to be draped across and nuzzled up against, to be
breathed on, then finger-painted in the marks of
things we might love to see appear in the murky circle
condensation briefly there then gone right back into
the cold, very cold air-conditioned atmosphere.

AGAINST ALL ODDS

Who will arrive, take hold of our hands
and explain it?
It may be an infant.
Where will it come from and where will
it be going?
From the wilderness of the heartland
maybe headed for New York City.
Will we learn to worship it?
Should we go and be near incunabula and animals?
Should we stare into its eyes
out of which all else pours?
And when we grow weary we should prop one another up.
And when we long for carelessness with what may we
slake it?
With the great poetry of Christopher Smart?
Should we read this poetry out loud
in front of the infant?
Perhaps the infant prefers the gentle John Clare?
And how should we address the infant?
With whispers, with staring?
Will we be able to shower the infant with gifts?
Maybe one gift, and may we give it and take it away
and give it again and again.
How else can we make ourselves worthy?
Is there nothing we can do?
We can buy as many silver rattles and cups and spoons
as our bank accounts can handle.
Oh, and take care to do so just as the full moon
begins to wane.
And when flocks of geese are not torn apart in the
storm-wrecked winds.

FOR A FEW SECONDS THERE I WAS A PANTHER

I looked like a woman looks
and words cruised paths through forests
and meadows and riverbeds and wind-whipped vaults
in my human cranium.
But they weren't the kind of words that ever live
to see the light of day.
And my hair remained hair
and my hands and feet did not change in appearance.
I did not grow fangs.
My nose stayed long and thin and my ears didn't move
to the crown of my skull.
Though now when I watch a panther lope over a ledge
below which a fawn sleeps by its mother I concentrate
on how much shows through its finest fur.
Back then, during the few seconds I was a panther,
I licked the panther's paw, I cleaned the panther's
nails, I combed the panther's hair.

CATHOLIC

You're creeping on your knees down the dark hall
on the lookout at all times for fanged serpents
dripping phosphorous poisons and you bump into something
tangible and neither you nor the tangible move.
Around the corner you two slither together
in a kind of danse macabre like a gruesome tango
celebrating the anniversary of somebody's death.
You're covered with so much paraphernalia it's a wonder
you don't just slump over. You've got your little whips
and big whips and your thorns and your chains
and your hot irons and your pokers and your sores
that smell like roses, you say, and wounds that come
and go as they please. You're pierced in so many places
your insides work like a grater and that hurts
your insides. On the bright side, when light streams
through you you can pass for a luminaria.
At the edge of a gray granite cliff
you and the tangible come to an impasse.
There's a struggle.
One of you slips and the other one stops its boot heel
on your fingertips, actually grinds its heel in your nails.
You're howling. Wolves are gathering.
Everything has gone oily.
Souls and ghosts and angels and saints are hunting you down.
You don't stand a chance in hell.
A little girl dressed in chicken feed sacks climbs up
beside you and offers you an ice-blue snow cone.
You reach for it. You fall.

GULLIBLE MOSQUITO

It's so unendingly grand
it stops me in my tracks.
I behave just like a baby jackass
butting its head against
an empty galvanized bucket.
Who'll be coming to fill it?
Someone with weather in his eyes,
lightning in one ear, smoke in the other.
A false door stays a false door
saying exactly what it was
put up on purpose for.
I should sit still in silence
for as long as it takes
a mosquito to hatch in a tear duct,
and red-winged blackbirds to nest in my pockets.
Should I call on St. Francis?
I should pull back to the rampant cattails
along the riverbank, part the muddy water,
plow through the riverbed, drill into
those famous tectonic plates and roil
around in all the hot stuff awhile
before boring out of the inner core.
I should picnic for strength
on the deep sea floor, pay my respects
to the crawfish's swimmerets
and the labial palps of the mollusks,
and ascend past the coral reefs,
drift beyond the continental shelf
whereupon, refreshed, tiptoe over
the bleached-white sand to a blanket
with a pillow on it. My broken pillow.

TRIBUTE TO CHARLES DARWIN FOR SOMEONE ELSE

I wish you would come back to life.
Could we have gone as far as we could go?
Thermals of thud-dry rocks and bones give off
an aroma of "the brain"—it is a tough puffball.
A few needles pause over Turkey Creek.
Is this how governments fail?
How in retrospect accidents aren't random?
"For that infraction stay inside
the invisible prison manufactured lies escape."
Look, it looks as if the people didn't want a rail-
road after all. In this we are nearly allied.
I wish you would come back to life.
Nearly windblown, nearly sulfurous.
Sulfur is pure yellow.
First we had no utensils then we had more
than we could use.
We couldn't remember their names.
Then we used just a few and wanted more.
We felt curious.
I wish you would come back to life.
You can't live in a cellar where no cellar
can be built.
That's just a name for it.
You can't hide from them forever.
Are you hiding?
I wish you would come back to life.
Wisps of the edges of your hair love the sun.
I've seen the sun worship your hair.

ASTRONOMY LAKE

She came in casting books from her sleeve,
She came in not shivering, casting books
Over the lake's surface, skipping books
To other shores.
He fell into the room by the lakeside
Upright straight through the crack
In the sky blue ceiling with his face exposed,
With his face on fire, crackling & smoking.
She stayed through eternity staring
Down past the many reflections cast
Over the water's surface, staring
Into the many thousand trails it appears
Snails have taken centuries to scrawl.
I am following systematic errors apace
In my human judgment, my human fragility,
My dizzy report. For those who believe
Evil travels in straight lines, for those
Who don't, who hold tight to good luck
Charms and say their prayers at night,
Not even did a poisonous snake dappled
In sunlight and shade find a straight &
Narrow way to its dinner. Someone says
We're quick to find patterns where perhaps
There are no patterns to be found.
She withdrew into the wilderness.
She asked him to make up a dozen myths.
He smote his face on the water.
He would not look at her.

A TRAILING-OFF OF ARGUMENTS IN PROSPECT OF LAMENTS IN THE GRAVEYARD OF UNFINISHED THINGS

Nothing would close in the commercial zones.
Through all the florid night the barn door banged
shut. No one could get up to put a stop to it.
Our mule took big, lonesome steps in her stall.
A bird went after a bird after a bird.
The fire would not start at all.
The runner never made it to third.
An undelivered note exploded and explained.
The tape just stuck in the midst of a joke.
A word to end all words refrained.
A green twig on a still pool twisted half an inch
then stopped. And with that dust demigods
made up ghosts, seeds scattered across headlines
drying on a side porch, cut-velvet blouse tossed
over a rosebush, kisses leaned into left hanging,
bowl of wrist deep bowl of water, first steps
skipped, first words intact, insane smiles
held up in snapshots, today all pinched up and
swaddled, tomorrow tricked out and upright,
someone with a birthmark and a cowlick,
with earlobes and a hairstyle, with questions.
Is it more than a continuum? Is it wrong?
Is it good? Where is it going? Can I come along?
Is it chiseled into stone? Will smoky *Phlebia*
and zoned velvet blue meet there with the trembling
merulius, the bristly parchment, and the radiating
teeth? Will it happen in the cool shadow of
a loveflash, with the usual upsets, in the midst
of holidays' aftermaths? Will someone see it?
Someone who worships a pony with a hobby,

who loves a rabbit with a talent, mice with
thumbprints, toy boats with brains?
Someone hiding and yawning and nodding.
Somebody along those lines, more or less
in that ballpark, saying along those lines,
baby doll, Beethoven is clearly dead, but you
and I, we're alive, something along those lines,
more or less, a ghost walking up the walk
with all the light of the western horizon strafing
through its hair, doing a little war shimmy,
a little come-hither honey I'm home.

THE NEXT STEP

We had been growing taller
and in compensation our feet grew longer
so that now our stairs no longer fit us
and we fell on them more often and our bones
broke so much we became crooked and funny
and our clothes no longer worked and our hats
could not stay on and we no longer fit in
our chairs with two arms and we no longer
knew what to do with the excess of elbows
but our knees now that we had so many of them
these we knew what to do with.

PERHAPS DIED & GONE TO HEAVEN

And when they rolled me over
great storms moved across my breasts
and a terrible accident lay on my ankles,
stories of extortion covered half my neck
and a birth announcement blazed across my face,
and when they turned me over
they found my back stamped with cryptic alphabets
and over the backs of my calves and thighs
they could just make out lines inscribed
in loving script they believed to be fragments
of stories children told of their fathers and mothers,
and when they searched past the roots of my hair
they felt the stirrings of a liquid music
and found the vault where lost objects are sent
and where words which are not spoken wait
and they turned back to their experiments
and their trials and left it.

A PERSONAL ESSAY: A PERSONAL WISH
TO FALL DOWN

The "falling down" part is fine
but not the fallen down
when all the broken feelings rush
to tell about their days
shoving one another around
shooting one another looks.
What a pity feelings have feelings, too.
You can wince when love looks away.
You can hear in a look.
As when a voice registers a timbre
into secret whispers.
As when a tree falls inside a closet.

A MODERN VERSION OF THE WAY THE ROSARY WAS ONCE SAID THROUGHOUT WESTERN EUROPE IN THE LATE MIDDLE AGES

I'm not sewing velvet patches on a woolen blanket,
not putting silver buttons back where they belong,
not sweeping or folding, not in my right mind,
not knowing that I owe or to whom I should
bow down or thank or praise, no, neither am
I putting aside, not storing up good deeds,
I'll need when I need bailing out, not putting
my house in order, no, not preparing
to meet my maker, no, nor do I wish to settle
old scores, no, not keeping wolves at bay,
and I'm not disturbing any beds, not in touch
with fine madness, no, I'm not crawling around
under a porch in search of a nest of puff adders
I hope not to find, no, I'm not skipping rocks,
nor counting how long it takes a ship's wake
to subside, nor waiting for the big one
to wash ashore and overwhelm its itty bitty
ancestors, no, I'm not trying to fathom a stew
of rotten flowers and rainwater I'm not pouring
from a vase at the left-hand back corner of a
freshly whitewashed tomb, no, I'm not getting
ready for company, not biting my tongue, though
a little bit of biting can feel good, not baring
my soul, I'm not hiding under the kitchen table
not wanting to listen anymore, not lost in a
camphor-reeking satchel inside a chifforobe,
not stretching under a bed on a cool linoleum
floor, no, I'm not sitting on top of a mule
surveying the sun and the moon, nor am I stirring

and stirring and stirring a roux, nor am I watching
strands of hot sugar fall into cool water, no,
I'm not climbing into a fig tree to be close
to mockingbirds and out of the way of hoop snakes,
and I'm not falling asleep next to a crate of melons
nor am I staying awake in case I might miss something,
no, I'm not staring forever into a fire,
nor walking through a rainstorm into a cypress
grove, no, and I'm not waiting for lightning
to strike, no, and I'm not pulling aside a
curtain so I can't see a man with a raccoon
looking over his shoulder or a woman holding
a cup of steaming coffee or hear what's passing
between them, or see a man at the end of a day
taking off his shoes, or a boy dressed in clerical
clothes dispensing frankincense, or a hand
shifting into reverse, or a hand turning numbers
to get into a safe, no, I'm not sitting on top
of a mule surveying the sun and the moon.

THREE

BALSAM OF MYRRH

Balsam of being here
With you and a thoughtful beetle,
With a sense of a wishful dime,
Who stood the sea on end and said
Go nap awhile in nigh egg room,
Get ye to some fish hatchery,
With your compass & passkey,
Your tin pitcher and bent cup,
Inside a cut a boy drew in his sleep
As he cut a slice of bread in his thumb,
By way of the several bridges a girl
Spends all night sweeping,
Red pears in pairs of ruby hands,
Oh, to be your sleeve, your shell,
Your lunar rover, your radial skin,
Your straw, your space suit, your neckline,
Your smoke working its way through a crack
In a skull, examining a breaking headline,
Ditchwater green hand grenades in pairs
Of identical hands, what did you do for
The twins and the sextuplets, is there nothing
You don't keep up your sleeve, you with all
The time in the world, bird with one wing.

LAST SYLLABLE OF RECORDED TIME

Remember the cloth cover, a scythe of red,
A blue membrane, green fingerprints, creases
Where creases need to be, where an eye can
Begin an education and twine, twine-binding
Keeping itself where it's wound, crossed, tied,
Deep inside a backroom's locker, our secret
Hiding place, lover, a room inside the water
Of a waterfall, behind our trick pilot's
Tailspin, inside a door between its keyhole
And doorknob, inside the second note in a
Boiling pot, where there's nothing left but
A drop of milk. One of those kinds of places,
It involves a ritual & a speechless messenger,
Blinding light and a sleep-talking sphinx,
Black smoke condensed on a sheet of glass.
We know exactly what it feels like and we don't
Know what it is.

AWE OF EVERYTHING

Do you know what's the unluckiest thing
In the world, a differential grasshopper
Said to me. I paused, I put down the
Diesel grinder I'd been trying to fix,
I turned off the stealth bomber, I faded
Away from the faded away pedals, I put up
Finely embroidered silk panels over the
Faces of the statues, I pulled the green
Vacillating amplifier into the hallway,
I swiveled seven of the chains and
Loosened the bolts in the balcony, I went
Into the barn to unlace the cattle and
Overturn the empty buckets, I put the
White flag on the mailbox, I cut the
Telephone wires, I fed the ducks better
Than I usually feed them, I adjusted the
Faucets so they'd drip a little, I waved
At old Mr. Wiley with his smokeless pipe
And his manpowered plow across the field,
I moved a clay pot off of a narrow ledge,
I taped the key to the bulldozer to the
Roof of the canopy, I took the cup of
Auger bits away from the rabbit hutch,
I put a padlock on the children's playhouse,
I picked up a stick by the sideyard gate,
I broke it over my knee, I went to the well
To fill a stone pitcher with cool water,
I let the donkey & the goats go. I took
A ladder to the hayloft and took down a
Suitcase. I could see across the valley
Down to the river from up there.

SEA FOAM

Tomorrow is today's perfect thought.
Saffron threaded through the central heating
System known as marrow.
God the Father's perfect thought, they say,
Turns out to be his son and later on our savior.
They say these jokers' first good long gander,
Instantaneous glances, one upon the other, arrive
With so much force what registers upon them is the
Holy Ghost, who later on will wield a tongue of fire,
And later on will bless us.
Tomorrow's perfect thought just begins to divide
Somewhere deep inside a drop of rain just now
Beginning to condense inside a cloud in someone's
Mind. The almighty love triangle mentioned above
Has gone on to greater things. Meanwhile it will
Have become apparent to my owner that it is high time
To take me down from my shelf and put me to good use.
But, alas, first I will need to be tuned.

AN ERROR LURKS IN SUCH A CERTAINTY

An eraser barks in South Carolina.
A bag of tickets blows into Nova Scotia.
A bottle of water circumnavigates the Maritimes.
A pencil sharpener ascends Mt. Everest.
A bus believes it is a thumbtack.
A baby turns itself inside out and nobody notices.
A pigeon assumes it has found all the answers.
Two doorways fall in love.
A broken-hearted drummer is confronted by a wind-
Shield wiper.
A train curls up on a couch cushion and dreams
It is stalking a squirrel.
A stick of butter dreams it is carrying a load of
Coal across the Badlands, in moonlight, on Monday.
A windmill gives birth to sixteen umbrellas.
A table fan reverses the course of a river.
A drill bit examines its conscience.
A plate of ribs invents perpetual motion.
A fishing pole replaces the Defense Department.
A piece of toast travels to Saturn.
A glove remarks on the beauty of sidewalks.
A cymbal explores the depths of an ocean.
A safety pin kisses a wolverine.
Some knee britches send out a round of apologies.
A crease saves the eyewitness from anthrax.
In the Earth's core a school of sunfish braid
Fine lariats for lovers of this world.

ENDLESS AFTERNOONS IN A SPRING ICE STORM
ON MOUNTAIN ROADS IN THE POCONOS

We followed a set of watery tire tracks through a series
Of dusty trails. We stayed nearby one another, we stuck
Next to the guardrails. Hoarfrost made an impression on
Us.

We followed the wet tire tracks along a dusty road until
We came to a railway crossing with lights flashing and
A bell ringing with no train coming. But we heard the horn's
Blast.

But we never saw it coming. On & off we talked about boxing
And who might be the next world featherweight champion,
Maybe the one with the eyes of an Egyptian prince, handsome
Muslim.

We went on in sleet and rain and fog up to where trees grew
Shorter by the hour and deer alongside the road were always
Dead and sometimes deader than we remembered deer could
Ever be.

We went up where charcoal stumps interrupted freezing pools
In places water froze. If there were views or vistas they
Were rumors clouds and mist poured over like tangled thoughts
Of lovers.

Off & on we talked about the lengths we go to pretend we're
Immortal and who might be the first of our kind to stumble
Upon one of the thousands of misplaced philosopher's stones
Very soon.

We followed where the road went between strafed granite walls
Weeping ice blue water with our eyes closed, with our thoughts
On cruise control, where the road rose and rose and we fell
In a cloud.

We went with the cloud without leaving the road as far as we
Could. We leaned closer to one another as the road went by.
We passed a doe & fawn eating by the side of the road where
Snow wasn't.

Off & on we talked about what happens when we love someone
Who doesn't love us. We figured in what happens to friends
When they go their separate ways. Soon we were mist, we were
Numb.

FUGUE PIROGUE ON BAYOU ST. JOHN

Reviviscence, what we call
Our destination, what we sew
Inside our hems, what we hew
With our oars into heavy waters,
With our poles exploring
Marshbeds, with chenier
To bump into.
Baby, baby, baby,
How our wake reaches
Back to the blue banks,
How our whimpers nose
Their way home,
How our fingers forget
What they've touched.
Winds ticking through live oak,
Through our hair lifting off
Our foreheads, our headlights
Pretending to be eyes,
Our terror-blinded, water-
Soaked wishes, what we say
To them when they die.

PRECIOUS CELESTIAL MEMBRANE

I'd fallen off my tricycle
And you said, good, do it again.
My echo chamber was filling with
Pure cane syrup, with eruptions
Of June bugs. I'd stared for 7
Hours straight at the hairs on a
Cricket's head. I think my head
Had a hole drilled in it. Slowly
It had been filled with starch.
A cranky old laundress was firing
Up her irons and thinking about
Pleats. Hyperspectrality washed
Over us and we washed over it.
You knew how much I liked to watch
Dusk creep around the planet.
You remembered how I'd sit for hours
On the riverbank waiting for something
To happen. You saw me standing behind
A fan listening to soundwaves break.
When I saw an ant crawling on your cuff
I touched my wrist, experts of the
Figure eight, ants of the expanding
Universe, eyeteeth of the renowned
Eternal life.

FEAR OF PSYCHIC SURGERY

His mother said she wished she'd never been born
So that he'd never been born so that now she would not
Have to kill herself. He says all this with a smile
Nodding as he tells us that his mother's still alive
And he's still doing what it was caused her to say
Such things to begin with. He says if he went looking
For an excuse to stop all he'd need to do is turn over
A rock. The rocker he's sitting in while he's talking
Creaks so hard all of us are afraid it's about to break
So he stands up to investigate and while it certainly
Is wobbly and one can see where it's been repeatedly
Repaired it doesn't appear he shouldn't sit back down
And continue with his story. He never mentions a
Father or anyone else in his family. He says he's
Been fleeing his hometown since the minute he was born,
If he hadn't gotten away he'd have done himself in.
Like mother, like son, one of us lamely jokes to which
He replies, yes, all the time we are extremely disinclined
Suicides. At which point one of us rears his head back
So hard it bounces off its nail and falls without breaking
At our feet. It's fine so we put it back where it belongs
And wait for him to get back to his story, but he wants
To think about the picture which is a drawing in charcoal
Of a pear and an apple overlapping without canceling one
Another out, a simple optical trick, a cool illusion,
He says, something that isn't that way and couldn't be
Otherwise. He says who needs excuses anyway. One of us
Agrees and accompanies assent with a somewhat exaggerated
Arm-length sweeping gesture. Across the room a white
Hyacinth tips out of its bowl onto the table. One of us
Is a witch's daughter but nobody tells him this.
Suddenly he asked for his coat. Suddenly we all stood up.

CONTRAST OF BLUES WITH AN ELEMENT OF ORANGE IN THE GOLDEN BRONZE OF CORN

At this time we still farmed
And hadn't yet finished

With our eyes.
It would be a while

Before we stopped wearing shoes.
Soul exchanges

Operated underground
Without regulation.

Have you ever been blindfolded
Without wanting to be seen?

We'd lived through nine utopia
And it showed.

We were promised
It would be the last time

We'd be turned inside out
Or reversed.

Some looked all right in silhouette,
Even outlined in orange.

There were still brides
And grooms of many different kinds.

A kiss was still
A kiss at this time.

INSTANCES OF WASTED INGENUITY

Falling off a triangle.
Putting two fighting fish in one bowl.
Talking yourself into a head cold.
Falling off a rectangle.
Putting insects in ice cubes.
Talking yourself out of doorways.
Falling off a parallelogram.
Talking into a microphone.
Falling off a footstool.
Putting earplugs in acorns.
Looking into a teacup for trouble.
Talking yourself out of breathing.
Taking a nap on a drum set.
Eating a peach with an air filter.
Wearing a dress made of hand grenades.
Talking a mudslide back up a mountain.
Lighting a campfire in a taxi stand.
Launching a boat on a horse trail.
Hiking in an elevator.
Falling into an envelope.
Discussing smuggling with customs officers.
Taking a cat to a dog show.
Falling in love with a toothache.
Questioning your thumbprint.
Looking for milk in a gas tank.
Kissing hydraulic acid.
Blindfolding a parking meter.
Falling over a water tower.
Reasoning with a baby.

WISHING THERE WERE SOME BETTER WAYS OF
EXPLAINING OURSELVES TO BIRDS

It's one o'clock in the ocean,
Nine in the morning on the nose of a mole,
Workday just beginning for carpenter ants,
Pencilsticks on holiday on a coral reef,
Sacred day for pants pockets, for handkerchiefs,
Anniversary of the invention of revolving doors,
Half-dreams that leave an impression walking
Through walls. It strikes me as strange when
Questions about birds have to do with whether
We can understand them. Sometimes a bird will
Look at me as if it has just read my mind or
As if it's wondering if I'll ever catch on.
Birds who've died crashing into glass walls
Come back to life as monks or nuns and every
Now & then as heavyweight championship boxers.
Does it snow where you are? Can you fry eggs?
Aren't our eyes strange, the way they stay open,
Then stay closed. Where did skinks get their
Bad reputations? When they're young their
Ornate blue and black markings make them easy
Pickings, then the ones who're left gradually
Turn brown as fine garden dust. It's one o'
Clock in the ocean. A slightly scarlet bullet
Races through a snowbank and lands on a sheet
Of black ice. A bird on its way to work notices,
Pauses, picks it up. What's happening on the
Golden Spike, who's touched it today?

THE GREAT DIVIDE

He's yours but I would put him high over
The Great Plains leaning hard against a window
Looking down from a few seats behind a prop's
Right wingspan. He belongs to you but I would
Have him watching a road cross several rivers
And veer off into farmland, into fall's display
Of green diluting into gold, browns, beige, and
Gray. I would have him follow a road into
Foothills along switchbacks to disappear in
Trees going up a mountain's east side and reappear
As it leaves the tree line behind and crosses
The Great Divide. A stewardess would offer him
A highball and a filtered cigarette and he would
Thank her and settle back into watching
Snowfields and in one of these he'd see a herd
Of elk and in another one nothing. He belongs to you
But I'd watch him lean nearly clean through
The window to follow a car he can see racing
Over a narrow bridge and that's when he'd remember
His father who chose never to learn to drive
Because he believed if he did he'd kill someone,
Because his father had done just that and was
On record in a record book high somewhere up in
The Alps as the first man to kill another human
Being with a car. He's yours and if I were you
I'd give him a name, a family, and a home.
I'd have him land near one of the big cities on
The West Coast and catch a train to a trolley line
And ride down to a port and sit on a bench

In front of where a small white fishing boat is
Docked. He'd tell a stranger sitting with him,
By his right side, he'd come to wait for his father.
Then he would close his eyes.

They were entertaining a serious argument
Concerning what they believed to be the dis-
Integration of the personal pronoun *I* as a
Viable sign for the self. A herd of mad
Bull elephants could be heard approaching
The city limits. Obviously they had all the
Time in the world. Rust was blossoming on
Them and they didn't notice it, but it was
Fascinating anyway. A boulder big as the
State of Texas was about to fall on the side-
Walk where they were talking but they were
In the midst of dismissing that curiously dis-
Integrating ironic lyrical *I*. A 9.5 on the
Richter scale earthquake was just getting
Started but they were stomping their feet
Saying I, I, I, and didn't really notice it.
Barbed wire clarity, one of them moaned.
Never self-celebratory, one of them sighed.
I was on my way to visit a good friend's
Grave, to visit a fox, box turtle, and a
String of buttons. But what really stung
Was how during all of their mind-bending
Ratiocinations and obsessed self-consultation
They never once mentioned "me."

HOT PURSUIT OF THE UNAPPROACHABLE

I'll not try to nail in a screw with an ice pick.
I'll not try to stitch an open wound with a fiddler's
Stick. I'll not try to write a prayer on a river
With flaming red lipstick, not try to find my way
Across the valley at night in a blizzard with a match-
Stick, try not to comb my hair with a walking stick,
Not give directions with a crooked stick, not put
Out a fire with two sticks, not keep a promise with
A broken stick. I won't ask the catbird to think
About nightingales. I won't complain to an ant that
It is so very small. I won't ask mourning doves
To change their tune, to be less skitterish.
I won't sing within earshot of anyone. I won't take
Up tightrope walking. I won't ask the dead to stop
Talking, to let me borrow their brooms. I won't say
To a scorpion you'd look better in cuff links, or ask
A tarantula to get a buzz cut. I won't ask the snake
What it overheard last week. I won't remind Chicago
What it was in the backtime or call Connecticut a
Corridor. I won't go into a bookstore and ask for a
Backhoe, or try to parallel park on an altar, or ask
For a splash of tears in my whiskey. I won't ask a
Zebra to blend in with baroque wallpaper or a great
Bengal tiger to lend its paws to a lawyer. I won't
Ask last year how it feels about tomorrow, or try to
Convince an oyster it has unlimited options, or talk
My pillow into believing what lies on it every night
Is a little less than the holy of holies.

SOUL MIGRATION

Down in a shallow pasture off Station Road
In a pre-evaporated afternoon
A redemptive scattering of bubbling clouds
Shallow quicksilver heat mirages
Pasture where blue fescue & chicory blue
Off and dusted with evening primrose pollen
Station-to-station pickup and delivery
Road less a road more a remote restoration
A second chance for shoelaces & shaving brushes
Small explosive devices of near resort
Herd instinct deactivated for now
Maybe forever will be arriving on time
Nine seconds late is just late enough
Head for the sky blue watering hole
Of who knew whom more will be known later
Horses can help out in most transactions
Has the slack been adjusted
Been partway to glory and back again
Blindfolded in a pasture off Station Road

Our streets filled with combines this fine
September afternoon, full moon inflated last
Evening. I went up with an air gauge to get
A reading. Poor moon, always under so much
Pressure. I looked down, a wisp of smoke
I saw rise from my true love's chimney.
After which inning do the stretching demonstrations
Begin? We played in the water tank all last night,
Displacing enough water to drown a whale, which is
Not something any one of us could stand to see go on,
Yet we had to admit not a one of us would know how
To stop it. And it would be so pointless.
Then you said let's talk about points.
Larry said the point would be to take care of someone
Nobody cared for. The baby's head had been pointy
For longer than anyone cared to admit. It's not
Pointy now but when it was it made a deep impression.
Lorraine said that's my point.
Gerard said he'd always pictured points in broad daylight
Though he knew he shouldn't be so pollyannaish.
Then he mentioned pencils, with a sheepish look on his face.
Baby said *no* is a very pointy word.
We all took deep breaths and submerged to see what we
Looked like underwater talking about points.
Then you said then what about progress?
Has there been any?
No one really wanted to talk about that, with their hair
All wet.
Baby said there was something moving around in his spaghetti.
He said it made him very happy.

The crazy priest threw holy water at the coffin
The way a frycook pops water on his grill to see
If it's fired up or not. But he spoke kindly
Of the man he'd come to bury. He took a long time
Telling the story of how Enoch & God liked to take
Long walks together. He spent a good deal of time
Naming the things they passed and admired, in their
Different ways. Things one wouldn't think Enoch or
God cared a hoot about. Old toasters rusting on
Ditchbanks—why were there so many of them, a book
Swollen with dew—who threw it down, a pocketbook
Turned inside out—had there been a crime, a dogleash
Hanging on a hemlock branch—a clue in a forgotten
Treasure hunt, the left foot of a pair of shoes—
The crazy priest threw holy water at the coffin
As if he were afraid of it. What if a miracle occurred
And the man inside the coffin came back to life?
What if the water were too holy? And when he walked
Around the coffin clattering holy smoke over it
He looked as if he wanted to flee and could not believe
His own eyes. But he spoke well of the man he'd come
To bury. He worked up to the time Enoch & God had
Been enjoying themselves so much they forgot the time
And found themselves closer to where God goes back to
When he leaves here. Now he closed his eyes.
He closed them too long.

NIGHTSHADE

I'm picturing your blood
Traveling through your fingertips
Up past your wrists.
One sick cookie, I think,
Or just another anybody
Toying with an idea,
Another someone out to scare
Oneself half to death.
I'm picturing the air glide
Into your lungs.
I'm seeing smoke explore
The empty spaces there.
Now I'm locking my eyes
And your eyes together
With my astonishingly soulful
Glue and adding on a padlock
And watching it rust and losing
The keys and should we meet up
On Crosspath Road I will say
It was meant to be, look at how
Our ankles look out for one another,
Look at how the nightshade vines
Reticulate in the mountain laurel,
Twisted brother.

Coionies of bees colonized our brains.
We could hear them buzzing in and out all day,
Bristling with pollens, loaded with nectar &
Sap. This was good we said, a kind of forti-
Fication. Honeycombs lent a delicate scaffolding
To platforms which otherwise might have been
Crumbling. On a mission, in a hurry, ace restorers
Sorted through everything scarlet, everything blue,
So many shades of green and brown, so many things
Faceted and flashing, hazels, roans and sorrels,
Hectic and fevered, steady and meek, backlog of
Ancient correspondence, bands of dedicated archivists
Traversing vast regions without signposts, back
And forth, without comment, into sublime, into
Ridiculous, without regret, among lost, cunning
And purely blank, from needle to thorn, from wake
Rocking onto shore to a field of fire, from out-
Right lies to words of consolation, from bows &
Arrows to buttons and bows to rags to riches, to
Buckwheat to broomsage to fescue to kumquat to
Avocado and back, and then they were gone.
Into this golden silence we lowered our spoons.

NINE SUNFLOWERS STANDING SEVEN FEET HIGH
WINTERING OVER IN A SNOWY FIELD

My love's mind has made me think
Of the direct path between a sunflower

And the sun, I've watched him be
The only un-sunflower in a field

Of sunflowers in full bloom,
When the hemisphere we happen to be in

Turns to look another way so as to see
More of the fathomless space we oar

And stars, I want to find a place
Where water is, to bring my love with me

There, put down the wooden crates
I carry with me everywhere, and say,

Let's have a seat and stay to watch
The moon come up from underneath the water,

Stars as far beneath the surface as
We can see, a satellite migrating

Among them, we'd follow its path
Directly into one another's souls.

It is a pincushion for darning needles.
It is an egg containing its brood.
It shares its nest with legions of Roman soldiers.
Perhaps it is over-inhabited.
It does not bite.
My head is a tabernacle, it loves the smell of frankincense.
If my head were a prison it would be empty.
It would be filled with the music of orange blossoms.
My head is a quiver, a patch and a satchel.
It is an arena.
My head is a satellite drifting out of its orbit.
Heads like mine have been found on all seven continents.
They have been linked to life on other planets.
They have been stamped on coins and traded for food.
My head is a nest of boxes, an overnight case.
It has been bombed and looted and sacked.
It has been riddled with scarves, with shoelaces.
My head is an unopened geode, an unopened coconut.
I like to listen to it slosh around.
I like to think of the moon working on it.
My head is a good hiding place, a safe house.
It is where to be in a lightning storm.
It is a cave curtained by a waterfall.

NOT THAT LAKE

Some lavender blue grayish sort of light lit up
In back of a row of lilacs quick as the lake
A few fingers near a silent switch of the lake
Up higher on a hill eleven or maybe lake
More than eleven tall antennae blinked lake
And unblinked day & night and who would want
To ignore all that said the lake
At first then there were the robber barons who the lake
And there were different kinds of birds by the lake
I could smell smoke of smoking eternally of the lake
I thought all of a sudden that I love the lake
I wanted to go over by the lake
Do you know wheat went out to sea by the lake
Do you know what went on when the lake
You get an inkling and then the lake
You begin to take a drink of water but the lake
You pay out a certain percentage over by the lake
You drift into other worlds and soon enough the lake
Your hand is like the lake
Your hair, the hair on your head, is the lake
I thought lake all of a sudden nearly in the lake
Those trees look weak in the knees for the lake
Gilded icons around the corner are for the lake
Someone's father old in his grave from the lake
Real honest-to-god choirboys singing for the lake
A belted kingfisher made occasional dives into a pond
Near the lake and a yellow-rumped warbler and a pair
Of northern shoveler ducks soon found rest by the lake
What someone thinks someone else remembers by the lake
Anyone will say almost anything to appear to be rational

Next to the lake
It was an exciting week inside the lake
Do you have any plans yet for the lake
Oh, all we needed was just a little bit more of the lake
Friday before last a little before five in the lake
Quick I'm shot through the heart please call the lake
I now pronounce you man and lake
The girl cut her teeth on the lake
The boy was named after his mother's side of the lake
After so many days of wind and rain the lake came out
And the lake was the way the lake was
And I put my hand on my love's knee under the lake
And my love's head turned and looked into the sea

BORDERLINE CASE OF INSUBSTANTIAL VACILLATING BREAKFAST SUSPENSE

It wasn't hard to see lines of direct attachment
strung up between each of the disparate parties
in attendance at the breakfast.
The baby said no hitting.
Invisibility enhanced and deepened their influence.
The baby whispered it's not your turn.
A transparent system of tunnels cluttered the place.
One could see in these all of the variously colored
trails of smoke accompanying feeling and thought.
The baby said crying won't get you anywhere.
One appeared to have become overly detached.
As if one inhabited the place as tenuously as a
recently inducted ghost.
The baby said now what do you say now.
Certainly there were words coming out of their mouths
and inside the words were billions of infinitesimal
bee-like engines of extraterrestrial origin.
The baby said that's not what you do with spoons.
Everything had at least a dozen hinges on it.
In order for all of the insides to be seen all of the
outsides had been erased.
The baby said no biting.
The technology was still in a fairly primitive state.
The baby said let's zero in on something.
If one emitted a standard interrogation such as
"could someone please pass over the aluminum pitcher
of ice-cold water without bubbles?" it registered.
The baby said let's triangulate a little longer.
Elsewhere appeared to be exactly where we were, its
latitude and longitude at last assigned, its

population not yet naturalized.
A universal solvent had been released in the area.
There was time to spare, baby said.
One at a time we disappear.

ROMANTIC

My love said take
All my books,

You can take all my clothes,
My hats, my shoes, my gloves,

You can have my watchband,
Take my sifters,

You can have my glass head
And my silver darts,

Take my wild boar, my astronaut,
You can have my pots & pans,

And my replica
Of the United States, and take,

While you're at it, all of the
Presidential figurines,

You can have all my matchbooks,
My binoculars, my exceptionally fine

Collection of cleaning products,
My one-of-a-kind snake-charming horn,

Take my sand dollars & beach glass,
Take all of my spices and salt & pepper,

You can have my smoked ham & brown mustard,
You can take away my Progresso soup,

Take away my bread, take my spoons,
You can have my sheets and my pillows,

Take my rugs and my three erasers,
Take my pitcher and the scarf you gave me,

Take my feathers my fox took
From my hawk, take my walking stick,

You can have my broom and my glass eye,
You can take away my atomic clock,

Take my dog, take my rule book,
Take my decoy and my bamboo cage,

You can take my girl waiting on
Her suitcase, my Michael Jackson doll,

You can take my mother and her priest
And their holy-water basin,

Take my drill and my hammer,
You can have all my brushes & combs,

Take my handkerchiefs and my scissors,
Take all of the keys you can find

In the house, take my scythe, my hoe,
My rags, my lamp with the lovers

Asleep in one another's arms, take
My sprite sitting on a stump daydreaming

Over an empty book, take my moose,
Take my coffee can of loose change,

Take all of my ant traps, take my
Windowpanes, take my steps and my doors,

Take my chicken shack & my wheelbarrow,
Take my combat ship plaque, take my

Vatican champagne flutes, my earplugs,
Take my quilts, take all of my quilts,

I would not take one stitch
Of one of your quilts, though I love them,

I sweetly interrupted.

EDGES IN CREASES

There went a wisp wasp on a leash with whiplash.
Everything in the backlash bank lacked rouge.
We'd take care of everything in the morning.
It is morning, isn't it morning, it's morning.
Thank you very much. Such as it is, red.
I wish there were more flambeaux everywhere.
It was better before the tuxedos exploded.
Twang, as in let fly love's pierciful arrows.
If it was tusks they wanted tusks it would be.
Swanking along without underbrush overhead.
Their beat, their dust, their sorry eyes.
You could see how deeply inspirational exhaustion
Bored some of them things, what are they called?
Lock of hair? Blue jar of gallstones? Stalemate?
There were nine glasses of milk lined up along.
I stayed inside a paperweight a fortnight.
I came out quarterly but lived too far away.
Feathers were flying. They discussed repaving
Their faces. My pajamas were sleeping
With one another in someone else's dreams.
Liars are more gullible than infants.
Liars are swimming gorgeous underwater.
Twice in one letter he wrote it was as if
A suicide found the water too cold.
He also said he saw the reaper below,
Between the iron bars of his cell.
He said there was more than enough room
In an asylum, he said what a queer thing
The touch is, the stroke of a brush.
He went looking to find who'd cut down
His fence. He was very proud of his sheep.

A WALK UP THE EVEN AND DOWN THE ODD SIDES
OF A STREET

A door you can get into a house through opens,
Down go your satchels & baskets & bushels,
A leaf's on the edge of a rug,
Bit by bit a staircase begins to make sense,
I had been looking too long into strangers' eyes
And I would make a note to stop doing that,
Some other time I could gaze, I could listen,
What's in your coat pocket tonight,
Were you thinking love's a demon reasoning,
How many ways were there for being around a table,
It hurts to watch words say things no one knows,
You went to sleep last night, most likely,
I did for a while,
I like it in there when something you want to keep
Follows you out,
A girl made two mistakes and she liked them both,
There was live ammunition in their heirlooms,
I saw a dozen owls in the space of two moons,
But they whoo-ed not for me more than twice,
For a while I adhered to a mailbox, a collection
Plate slid down the aisle, columns of numbers
Had been penciled in the margins, I was allowed
To put up a white flag so the country doctor
Could come and find us,
He boiled his needles in a little enamel pot,,
He wiped steam from his eyeglasses with a corner
Of the tail of his dirty white shirt.

CORD OF WOOD, SPARK OF SHOES

For a while in back of stepped aside in case not even close
Still wanted a better view and this worked for a while until
Something someone said changed the terms in favor of after all
This time and all of a sudden wanted to start over with as soon
As possible after almost out of sight returned with someone
Thought better of it almost too late to make much difference
And for a while nothing went on but some sighs and a couple of
Gasps now and then found in an out-of-the-way place second
Thoughts were having profound effects in the first place or
At least after too close to call backed off without how could
It be to begin with and found something someone touched under
Somehow something must have mattered slowly returning almost
As if nothing had happened and as if nothing else at least
For the time being could possibly be more important than that
And is so everything would have to be might come around more
And more often and forever might reverse itself at last time
This happened it wasn't what anyone thought it was really wanted
It to be not that that mattered so much and would for a while.

Then find out who picked apart the Badlands
And made them beautiful.
What do you want to know about armbands?
Tell me something to do with time.
Who picked out blue, who coiled smoke?
Make a list of anything you've ever thrown
Into a river, peach pit, bones, broken mirror,
Wedding band, telephone, tape recorder, nails,
Staple gun, empty cans, a heavy suitcase, a
Worn-out hammer, etc., something you wrote
And sealed inside a bottle, something you
Couldn't say to anyone else. Who signed
Your birth certificate? Were you born
A dust storm, do you remember the doctor's
Hands? Who said a little too much is enough
For me? Make a list of anything
More than two of. Make a list of nothing
You've ever borrowed. Who wound rope?
Find out where the pocketknife went.
Find out why the hunter put an elk's head
In the black oak. Who picked out livid violet?
Find out who owns everyone's water rights.
What happened around the blue baize table?
Who donned a dusty apron and dirty cotton shirt?
Who made a mundane glory in the precincts of the
Arena? Find out why if magnetic resonance
Imaging changes quantum states patients emerge
Seemingly unchanged. When will the path past
The churchyard be filled with cherry blossoms?
What's behind the green door? What's with the
Hysterical fugues? Why is mad-traveling the

Most "natural" way to be insane? Find out who
Was creeping around "mental hygiene." Why
Was a customer afraid to leave the pharmacy?
Find out a way to be invisible.
Not like a ghost, find a way around that.

TAME SWANS

The gristmill's gone
Though the river isn't

An oak's been quartered and drawn
And carted to town and stacked

In two cords on the edge of a lawn
There were eggs in the air

Most of them didn't break
There was a suitcase patched

In three places with black duct tape
Waiting at the bottom of a staircase

When it's cold outside it's not a good idea
To be inside standing by a window breathing on it

A message arrived as a rocket ship flies
There was a menacing kindness in the eyes of a stranger

A note of alarm in the voice of a neighbor
A nuthatch looking at itself in an invisible mirror

Every other house was empty
Every other house had someone living in it

The flags were all gone
But the wind wasn't

For a while no one missed leaves
For a long time everything was a blur.

A TANGO WE NEGOTIATED TO TURN OUR
TRAIN AROUND

Irony is about killing your father, blinding
Yourself, and sleeping with your mother, not
Necessarily in that order. It haunts the ice
Cone a wise-eyed baby licks in the zoo house
While it watches a gorilla suck on a tick it's
Just pulled from its neck. A periscope is one
Of the funniest sights in the world and one of
The most unironic. A periscope would not know
Irony if it came up and bit its nose off. Radar
Isn't ironic either, but for different reasons.
There's something about having a personal rela-
Tionship with God that seems sort of ironic but
Perhaps isn't. In the year 2000 there were 2,000
Tigers in the U.S. state of Texas. A travesty,
Most likely, though not ironically. An American
Couple deciding to marry on Bora-Bora in a tra-
Ditional Tahitian ceremony should involve some
Kind of irony but apparently didn't. The thrill
With which the young man from Prague whipped
Potatoes was catching and definitely not ironic.
Sometimes someone's forehead will seem to have
Scars on it where its antlers have been removed.

THE COLD WAR

I suppose I wanted an ice pick.
Or it wanted me and who am I late in the afternoon
could have fooled an assembly of interrogators.
A fawn had walked across the lawn.
I'd been chilled to the bone.
One of them said we could do without spoons.
One threw rocks and one threw stones.
One took the money and ran.
One had a pail and one had a bucket.
Suppose what we did was maim the Holy Grail?
On purpose, by accident to keep an even keel.
I don't think the moon plays favorites.
I don't think we resemble bees.
Suppose we had to do without roses.
What's the difference that it really happened?
I did what I was told and stayed with the horses.
We lived together on a floating island.
Do you remember what happened with the floating baby?
Do you remember what we hid and why it was hidden?
Does it matter what could never be found?
If we'd found it would we have put it in practice?
One of them trained an oak to grow up a lattice.
I'm in awe of involuntary muscles.
Is there anything better than photosynthesis?
I did what I was told and slept with the fish.
We lived together in a cold cracked place.
Do you remember where you hid a block of hot ice?
Do you remember what the blankets were for?
A dog disappeared in a basket of fog.
I don't think we resemble dogs.
I hid inside a footprint and did what I was told.
Nothing didn't really happen I suppose.

IDIOGRAPHIC

Lawns scattered with ghosts, with clothes on,
Ghosts who shouldn't be waving wave anyway
And their arms fall off. They float away.
Ghosts with party hats, with tape measures.
One with a shovel looking for a grave digger,
One with a funnel looking for a little to add
To a lot, one with a pocket full of quarters
With a soft spot for parking meters, one with
An unforgettable story about an exuberant dachs-
Hund, one with a cursed dowry, with a whimsical
Yet profound look at atomic medicine, one with
Outstanding genealogy, one with answered prayers,
One on a jag analyzing recent political peccadilloes
In light of biblical prophecy, eye-opening & disturbing,
That one, one with a full set of teeth looking for an
Open mouth, one with a branding iron in search of a
Soul mate, one with a skeleton key looking for an unlocked
House, one with an ax looking for a block of ice, one
With a can of gasoline and a box of kitchen matches, one
With a mallet looking for a wicket, one with a dozen eggs
Looking for a henhouse, one with milk looking for a milk-
Ing barn, one with a cup of water looking for a river,
One with a dictionary searching for a library, one with
Loops of rope looking for a field of hemp, one with a
Searchlight, one with a wounded snake, one with a vat of
Permanent white dye, one with a sweat, one with a nose-
Bleed, one short of breath, one with a hairbrush, one with
A comb, one with a full head of hair, one with a foghorn,
One with perfume on, one walking through a town banging a
Bone on the sweet side of a snare drum.

FOUR

prologue: *a stick, a cup, a bowl, a comb*

These were some of their laws:

These were a few of the miles they cruised:

Here is where their beds went down:

With this their fate was sealed:

These are some things they shared:

These were with what they were comforted:

In this manner were they made to be cared for:

In these ways were they shaped to be seen:

Among these things were what they could bear:

In this time here is what they will be shown:

With this will they be remembered:

These were some of their customs:

These were with what they kept to themselves:

Here is a place they questioned:

In this way were they asked to provide:

These were what they provided:

In these instances thus were they praised:

It was with this were they wondering:

These were with what they marked themselves:

With this will they be never forgotten:

These were some of their means:

Here is an example of one of their methods:

With this did they solace themselves:

With this did they adorn themselves:

In these ways did they keep their provisions:

This is what they did with what they were fond of:

By this practice did they shore up magnificence:

These were what they were asked to furnish:

They caused these things to be memorized:

These were their most common rituals:

Among these these were considered unnecessary:

And in these were they in surplus:

These things they misused:

And prized:

And forfeited:

And pitied:

By these means did they resist their discovery:

These were some of the choices they made:

With these did they choose to be represented:

With these did they divine:

And with this were they occupied:

With these things did they labor:

For these things did they hope:

For these did they say they would die for:

These were the bargains they struck:

This is what they were given in exchange:

This is how they recognized one another:

By these means was love aroused:

Here are fragments of what they worshipped:

Among these things they passed their days:

Here is what they were willing to sacrifice:

In the traces of these things they were known by:

This is what they have left:

Here is where they left without a trace:

These were some of their gifts:

(and then it moves back in at the end of the day)
(they're sundogs) (there's no way to catch one)
(you don't do anything, you try to look like a
rubberneck) (you try not to put a horse there)
(those are pronghorns) (why can't they be ante-
lopes) (we were walking inside a duststorm)
(you were born in a duststorm) (you say so as if
it means something) (it blew in some magpies)
(it came in under the doorframes) (we were migrating)

(you rolled up the blueprints) (you rolled up the
sidewalks) (it's a gametrail) (like biofeedback)
(it looks as if it used to be somebody's backyard)
(it's covered with lawnmowers) (that's a solution)
(like bentwood) (like an arroyo) (after a flash
flood) (that's where we went to find arrowheads)
(it was a reflex) (as if someone had hammered its
kneecaps) (they were always saying they weren't
saying what they were saying) (it made it hard to

follow them) (they were telling us they had to make
up their own minds) (it looked like an enclave)
(it wasn't a sewing bee) (they said we'd just have
to believe whatever it was they wanted us to)
(it looks as if it used to be a ballfield) (all
that's left is a little slice of rubber)
(it was a slider) (that's a place to put the side-
lines) (that's a line drawn in a basin of water)
(we needed a better light source) (we needed

sugarcane) (we needed our caneknives) (we needed
dry blankets) (we couldn't get away from the under-
currents) (they were everywhere) (they were thick
as thieves) (they never seemed to mind that) (you
said they are what they are) (like a tarpatch)
(it sounded as if someone were cranking in a really
old fishing line) (but it was amplified) (like it
was prehistoric) (it was their paydirt) (they
wanted to put it in vending machines) (we would

be paying for it with our shirts) (and with our
pith) (that's what happens to cattle) (they call
it a necklace for short) (what if you resist be-
lieving that) (they'll say you're an ephebe)
(they'll say you reek of colostrum) (like jaw-
breakers) (like seesaws) (you'll be booby-
trapped) (you'll wish we were sunspots) (that's
how we got here) (it was written all over the
asphalt) (we needed someone to translate)

(something that was necessary) (not because they
had nothing to say) (or maybe they were afraid to
say it) (maybe they were afraid it would be too
costly) (I doubt it) (it seemed to be antiseptic)
(too antiseptic, it killed everything) (that is
an exaggeration) (it was a flare up) (it was a
flamethrower's decoy) (it's written all over a
wristband) (you came in bobbing around) (you called
it dancing) (you ricocheted because you had to)

(there was still dew on the grass) (you were
frisky) (if you want to call it that) (everyone
was frisking everybody) (they said it felt good)
(they were practicing a new kind of hero worship)
(it was deep-fried) (we needed to be decapods)
(we were supposed to roll with the punches) (as
though we were boiling) (as though we needed to
be) (so say you're some kind of star) (become
angry) (don't let them take your picture) (be

sullen) (feel as if no one understands you)
(it looked as if it were some kind of dealership)
(so we deviated) (we variegated) (you were the
marshal of that parade) (we took over a convent)
(we didn't stencil) (we were rifle birds) (you
said we were ordinary people) (we didn't like fly-
paper) (we had a few yardsticks) (we needed to
reconnoiter) (you were the one who could go in
and out of the house without notice) (you were

noiseless) (you were never baptized) (there were
several other options) (we needed to spend a
night in a cypress grove) (like bloodhounds)
(you were self-propelled) (like a distributary)
(when a thought flickered over your face)
(when you ran a hand through your hair)
(when headlights crossed over your cheekbones)
(when you shifted away to look into something)
(you were the one with oars in your hands)

144

(overtaken by night) (is all that happened) (just as
it did every evening) (as in those belated obsolete
times) (that was when a mouse slinked down the shadows
alongside a wall to its tiny little rooms to obsess
every night over its fear of growing larger) (there
are worse phobias) (fears of going to bed at night)
(of ice and music and birds and flutes and money)
(fear of swallowing) (of being wrong) (fear of not)
(understanding) (of missing out on something)

(whenever a certain one said *aggravation*) (it was
hard not to be put in mind of an auger) (in a gravel
pit) (with a mind of its own) (hard at work grinding)
(up all the words in the world) (and not of one small
pebble in the heel of a sock) (I remembered when
it became clear) (that sounding like a broken record)
(didn't mean I'd done something) (really very exciting)
(and it sounded like some kind of mania) (like the one
about the 2nd Coming of Christ) (or joy in complaining)

(remember how it used to be possible) (to make every
singer sound like a mouse) (by adjusting the speed of
a turntable) (that was aggravating) (and is obsolete)
(and who do we have to thank) (if words are shadows
as some say they are) (and they do not look like shadows)
(while they lie on a page) (what is the light that)
(doesn't pass through) (invisible things) (these words
must be) (or something like that) (I overheard last night)
(it's probably ambergris) (or isinglass) (or lacecloth)

(it feels pretty good to shimmy) (but it can look
like a frenzy) (now I find out just a little too late
phrenology's the science of teaching men how to
phrenologize without their knowing) (to size up
their inclinations and measure their vanities) (or
lusts) (or compassions or cares) (or obsessions or fears)
(sooner or later the mouse is going to miche back
out of its house) (and perhaps lavish in the fields)
(it was semi-private) (semi-peaceful) (semi-romantic)

(it was almost impossible) (not to start misdemeaning)
(once we got to the mezzanine) (overtaken by night)
(where so many mind readers were milling around) (it
was all one could do) (not to perish the thought) (to
profess one knows someone else's thoughts) (some-
one's semi-private thoughts) (I guess, is so out-
landish) (it's understandable it would be fashionable)
(too much overbrowsing was driving all of the second-
guessing farther) (and farther) (into the wilderness)

(a fellow told me this morning) (some bears are so shy)
(they walk backwards) (to avoid meeting people) (they
walk backwards in their own tracks to go where they
want to get) (and that's understandable though it
seems it would be overaggravating) (to any reasonable
bear) (a rock jockey told me there's a bear in her
woods who likes to come up to the house and stare)
(through her windows) (it's another way they have
of turning the tables) (and a curious look is charming)

(as is a look of candor) (and a camelhair jacket)
(an ex-fisherman I know who's become a weaver
and is a keeper of camels says once a camel gets
to know you it will remember you forever) (and
it will know everything there is to know about
your character) (so be careful) (so be careless)
(or cautious) (or mutinous or mountainous) (but don't
be a miser) (fear of money is what that amounts to)
(whatnot to fear that) (there is nothing to fear)

(overtaken by night) (just a little belated) (one
hopes there will still be room) (at the table)
(I'm thinking of the table with these thoughts
on it) (layers of candlewax and fallen
petals) (a moose with a broken antler) (a worn out
elf with a curious look on its face) (a girl pre-
tending she's reading a book) (a brave-looking goat)
(who's waiting to have its legs delivered) (a tiny
skull with its regions marked off) (a monkey on

wheels) (three gold mice as small as grains of rice)
(eating poppyseeds) (a pair of farmers in their go-to-
town clothes) (sitting in a field) (a red-winged blackbird)
(a pelican) (a condor) (a finch) (a fork someone's bent)
(a bowl someone's used) (a stack of news of the day and
yesterday and the day before) (that and the day before
that) (if you think when I'm reading I'm reading) (to send
what I'm thinking) (along for the ride) (you're right about
that) (like a pebble in the auger of its mania)

(none of them are where we left them)
(maybe the wind blew them somewhere)
(they were fond of traffic circles) (they built them)
(it was one way of thinking) (but you can't get
very far) (if you stay on a circle forever)
(well) (it feels less certain than crossing a bridge)
(that's a poker face) (it's a soundless soundtruck)
(nobody can find the bottom of that)
(we were standing aside) (we had a viaduct)

(it went around and around hard by an edge of the
rotary) (we could cover it with a pavilion)
(we could distract it with fire birds)
(they were just kids then) (they saluted for the fun
of it)
(they did it with true fidelity) (like pitchforks)
(they tramped right through their firedrills)
(tramped after the bombscares)
(tramped over their sidewalks) (they did it freehand)

(they didn't even have any guiding stars)
(they didn't even have a full set of funnels)
(they would have to be impromptu) (like glaciers)
(maybe they would find a few handbooks)
(they'd need a squadron of thaumaturges)
(it was slivovitz) (it took out the guesswork)
(that's not translation) (why would it need to be
transmogrified) (it was already ugly enough)
(it was slick) (it was pulp) (they were pawns)

(they said they were illuminati)
(we were never given back our hat pins)
(so they sent it off to the rendering house)
(when it came back) (there wouldn't be much there)
(of what it once was) (you wouldn't be able to
recognize it) (they said they were traveling
salesmen) (they were dissimulators) (they sold
bywords) (like bunco artists) (they were in thrall
to officialdom) (it was hackwork)

(and they were very small cotyledons)
(their axis of revolution was not there)
(they had no axis of symmetry) (it was confusing)
(it was like having a series of too many concussions)
(we were stuck in a go-between situation)
(the rumors came down the mountains)
(it was the world's tallest waterfall)
(in other words it was twicetold)
(it was siltwork, it was sudsy, it was frothful)

(it never felt right to feel like a by-product)
(we took the causeway) (it was longer)
(we could wait for things to transfigure)
(we could look) (for sound advice) (we could sit
under a hemlock in a windstorm and listen)
(we could go stay by some wetlands)
(we've already tried that)
(it was bedlam)
(we left with our eardrums blistered)

(we looked corrugated) (like we were washboards)
(what did they mean by nipped in the bud)
(you're not left with a leg to stand on)
(that's submissive) (that's not salty)
(we could go back to the bayou we came from)
(it's not there anymore) (it's been excised)
(that had some kind of filthy lucre in it)
(whose was it) (it didn't belong to anybody)
(that was all pretend) (like psameads)

(you could see there was part of a stigma)
(it had fallen over) (maybe somebody pushed it)
(were the requiems for it) (there was dark matter)
(we felt as if we were running right beside you)
(we were side by side) (like eyebrows)
(but we couldn't see where we were going)
(we needed our sea legs) (we needed some freesia)
(say you're press agents, show them your flack)
(now filibuster for as long as it takes)

(do some drumbeating) (be immutable) (rend some
garments) (be hardcore) (show some compassion)
(put something out of its misery) (misrender a
little ambivalence) (send it on ice skates)
(it looked trampled) (it wasn't impartial)
(you could see where it was scorched and a trace
of what it was scorched with) (it was ephemera)
(just past the traffic circle comes a penitentiary)
(they say it's empty) (that means it's teeming with life)

(we were subterranean then) (it lasted a long time)
(you wore a jacklight) (like a third eye)
(we were spelunkers) (we worked in the crypts)
(and the icemines and the saltmines and the
sewers) (remember the raft we took down there)
(and up in the mountains where the silvermines were)
(remember the time we rounded a corner right in the
middle of a gunbattle) (only one side had guns)
(the other side were birds) (they were pigeons)

(what were pigeons doing roosting underground)
(being shot down from rafters)
(they said it was target practice) (they said they
were killing a little time) (they were good at it)
(who were they) (they were armed guards)
(what were they guarding)
(they were in uniform) (they wouldn't tell us)
(they did it for kicks) (it was a perk) (they were
just parked there) (like a kickback)

(sometimes when you walked behind me you made me
doubt my own shadow) (that was not on purpose)
(it was tangential) (not like a bonus)
(we said we were sightseeing) (we said we had
jetlag) (we showed them our strip maps) (we gave
them our passports) (we said we were on our way
to some kind of shivaree) (we needed a sidewalk)
(we said we were shirring) (we said we would shunt
it) (one of us said we were sorry) (we were jerry-

built) (we were tempest-tossed) (we were crusta-
cean) (we needed a shrimp boat) (we'd take a sub-
lease) (we would be temporary) (we still had our
cubicles) (they'd lifted the quarantine) (not in
the dockyards) (we needed a shade tree)
(that was their shoptalk) (we didn't know it)
(maybe we said jamboree) (like a side bet)
(there was so much cryptic gossip down there) (we
needed a speedboat) (to keep up with it)

(we needed some oxygen tanks) (we needed gas masks)
(there wasn't much of a cover charge)
(it was an earthquake)
(it was melodramatic)
(we felt like a lost cause)
(it was like being a bee stuck in an icecave)
(subsequently) (that's what we'll be)
(it was May 14, 1804) (we mounted our gondolas)
(we unfurled our telescope)

(something I really needed) (got left behind in a
cubbyhole) (but you took it in stride) (like a
parakeet) (like a dice cup)
(not even telekinesis could fix it)
(we'd stored what we'd need) (it was waterproofed)
(it was bone brown) (it was café au lait)
(no) (more like honey) (the dark kind)
(they were paper wasps)
(they were extremely social)

(they made paper) (they didn't make honey)
(say you're a printer) (say you like dingbats)
(start with a bible) (or something like that)
(say you're bogged down in a dialectical mind-
shaft) (say minefield) (roll up your windshield)
(make it a paradox)
(say it's a telethon) (point to the overpass)
(say it's a subsidiary) (not your main line of
work) (that's how you cover your back)

(with a paper fan) (no less)
(technically it isn't raining) (rain doesn't
happen in these parts)
(it isn't wind) (it's a vacuum)
(like the sunny side) (like a vortex)
(do you think it might be surmountable)
(it is possibly all blue retractable)
(maybe with some kind of hydrofoil)
(that isn't fog) (I don't know what it is)

(it looks like some kind of cover-up)
(as soon as you get to the tunnel start whistling)
(not literally under the volcano) (under its influ-
ence)
(someone said they were mutant royalists)
(that's not the call of the wild) (that's a calliope)
(you can hear it) (it's way off in the distance)
(the eels were pretty friendly when they twined around
our fingers) (that) (that brings to mind a calf's tongue)

(some of them stay underground for seventeen years)
(they emerge singing) (if you can call that singing)
(they leave their husks) (clinging to treetrunks)
(we call them ghostbirds)
(we call them glassphantoms)
(if you can stand to you can crush some and drink
them) (but only with rainwater) (you've collected in
a babyshoe) (and the baby had better be living)
(and you should be standing by a spider lily)

(it's a natural progression from roustabout to
roughneck) (it was like being forwarded)
(you felt as if you were being passed from one hand
to another) (but it wasn't a race) (you weren't a
stick) (it was a way to keep body and soul together)
(if you say so) (it was like sweeping sand on a
sanddune) (you didn't do it for money) (it was spo-
radic) (like a forte) (it didn't seem to do much)
(it could barely keep the wolves from the door)

(they were tight-knit) (it was only natural they'd
be in-grown) (once they were shunned they were shun-
ned for good) (remember what happened when the lode-
star was forsworn) (we were spellbound) (like a round-
house) (it sounded like some kind of chemical) (like
an insecticide) (was it uxoricide) (it almost was)
(they had no sense of valence then)
(they were not splicers)
(they almost never remembered to shut their scissors)

(we were close to a lumberyard) (you could smell
it)
(we made pretty good use of their pallets and fork-
lifts)
(it was how we lived) (we were wayfaring)
(sometimes we were free-floating wicks)
(we could see what we needed) (it was always far off
in the distance)
(out of reach)

(like virga)
(like something you want in a fable)
(you can drag a table up to where you think it is)
(you can stand on it)
(you can have a friend nearby spot you)
(somehow or other)
(you can pretend you don't want it)
(you can make like you're looking for cobwebs)
(as if you're putting a key on a ledge of a doorframe)

(everyone felt feeble for a few days) (or in apogee)
(we needed a switchback) (like a cowpath)
(it was riversand) (it was slippery)
(the keynote address lacked a keystone)
(like an avalanche) (remember the mudslide that al-
most killed us) (we were lucky that day) (we'd been
fishing) (we were fishers though we didn't know it)
(and we were not nearly as superstitious)
(that's why my shirt's) (on inside out) (it has to stay

that way until we get to the floodplain)
(do you think we'll find the highway)
(you can say you're a wrangler) (try to look
windblown) (show them your roughhewn manners)
(show them your bowlegs) (say what you can do
with numbers) (keep them busy)
(give them your business card) (if you have one)
(point them to a brick sidewalk)
(show them your brick)

(do you remember why they pounded bricks into dust)
(was it for some kind of solstice)
(I don't think I ever knew what they were doing)
(we should try to make it to an esplanade) (maybe
we'll find who's sending distress calls)
(it was a wet blanket) (it had gone overboard)
(sometimes they were almost good providers)
(we can use my necklace) (the one of buffalo nickels)
(how come we've never seen you wear it)

(it weighs a ton) (like an iceberg)
(the unwritten laws turned out to be the worst kind)
(they were all about vengeance)
(say you were shipwrecked) (show them one of every-
thing) (show them your lean-to) (let them see you
all tattered) (some of the icebergs are melting)
(what's going on with the subscriptions)
(the sun still had the wherewithal) (it was coaxing)
(four o 'clocks to open) (they were relaxing)

(the ground was sliding away from under us)
(there were ten-foot poles touching us everywhere)
(as if we'd been caught in a hailstorm)
(with our guard down) (on a proving ground)
(it was rocky) (we were shaky) (we felt like
ice cubes) (there was no lair there) (we had no
den then) (there were too many collars)
(we slipped them) (we left them where no one
could find them) (especially we couldn't find

them) (I thought you said we didn't want them)
(we were welders then) (we made sparks fly)
(our masks turned us into some kind of insects)
(we were ants then) (we were straightforward)
(we were dirt-movers) (we were good bone-cleaners)
(we were praying mantises) (we were efficient)
(we were cannibals) (it was uncanny) (we were
at the mercy of tactical angels) (they were
vigilantes) (they were zealots) (they threw

zeros around like crazy) (like they were collars)
(it's a cabinet) (so open it) (open it slowly)
(it's filled with bottles) (they're filled with
liquids) (liquids are for strangers) (they wanted
to claim their ancestors) (they wanted to walk
one behind the other) (they wanted to stand side
by side) (to be in a bucket brigade) (but there
was no flood) (there was no fire) (they were building
pyramids) (they were mining for something) (they'd

had their brains sealed) (that was a near miss)
(this amounts to a kind of immunization) (it's a
homeopath's dream scheme) (it smells like rocket
fuel) (keep your flints down) (don't say any-
thing incendiary) (there where there's cant there)
(there was little cantabile about it) (they
weren't singing) (they were storing up ammunition)
(it was a kind of status-seeking) (they were
lever beavers) (their dens were very complicated)

(and their plans were all for sale) (we need
some cantilevers) (we need to alleviate something)
(we are going down in an elevator) (this is a
close shave) (it wasn't as if we appeared out of
nowhere) (it was a mindset) (they were all roosters)
(they'll end up in stewpots) (just one will be left)
(just one booster rooster) (bringing the sun up)
(lighting the sky) (so we can see one another)
(so our skin can change colors) (so we can walk

under umbrellas) (so we can reactivate the parasols)
(we need some shade trees) (we need chinaberries) (we
need a mimosa) (with its pink sticky flowers)
(and good limbs to roost on) (and its fizz frenzy)
(and its riot gear) (and its ultracanonical security)
(it was a club then) (it was all claviform)
(they were clucking) (like they were brooding)
(we were in very close quarters) (like they were
clubable) (we needed a keyboard) (we needed some

soul-stirring music) (they were all out of
anthems) (they were fighting over the inheritance)
(they wanted the baubles) (they wanted the homestead)
(it was like being tangled in under a Portuguese
man-of-war) (with stingrays for company) (and you
hadn't had any choice in the matter) (they bap-
tized the dead) (they clubbed baby seals) (they
were motherfuckers) (and what's the corollary
to that) (we were better off being orphans)

(not knowing where we came from) (to whom we owed
allegiance) (where we got our sharp clavicles from)
(it was a posse) (the dispatch was summary) (we
were down-and-out) (we were on the streets) (we
were blistered) (we were stonewalled) (they
kept sheep in us) (and snakes liked to lie in the
sun on us) (and ants and spiders and centipedes
went in and out of us) (we were permeable)
(we had gooseflesh) (we were acting like stoics)

(you never learned to ride a bicycle) (you were
stubborn) (you were born that way) (it made you
beautiful) (like ants in amber) (that was a
necklace too hard to wear) (it weighed more than
a cinderblock collar) (you couldn't fly with it)
(you couldn't float on your back all day on a pond
with it on) (you couldn't run as fast as you
wanted to when you were with it) (it took justice
into its own hands) (suspiciously) (like an octopus)

(might as well be ironing) (a complicated
blouse) (or sorting seeds) (you could be
watching) (I could be walking) (in a daze)
(in a cemetery) (scattered in the woods)
(you could be in there) (hiding) (it would
be just as well) (to be unstitching thread)
(from a perfectly hand-stitched hem) (count-
ing) (something that doesn't) (need to be
counted) (combing through things) (needing

no combing) (untangling) (something already
untangled) (we could be in a boat then) (we
would have been fishing) (we'd be in a swamp
there) (in one of its channels) (with cypress
trees everywhere around us) (it would be
almost dusk now) (we'd be surrounded) (by
owls) (they'd be looking) (as if they couldn't
see us) (that's when our line broke) (we had
to leave it) (we couldn't take it with us)

(we left it behind) (it was abandoned) (for-
gotten) (no use to us anymore) (an obstacle)
(a barricade) (a battery) (of too many ques-
tions) (we didn't tell them) (where we were
sleeping) (what we were doing) (we didn't say)
(what they wanted to hear) (we kept our own
counsel) (we unlearned their language) (we
turned off our recognition meters) (we went
back to zero) (before that) (we were negative

numbers) (we were useful) (we were a way
around) (very many contradictions) (we were
like circles) (we were overlapping) (one
another) (we were looking for similarities)
(wherever we looked) (we would find them)
(saying good-bye) (in the morning) (snow
would be all over everything) (all they'd
leave were their footprints) (wind would
blow them away) (in fine smoking sheets

over highways) (in sandsmoke moving
over some beachheads) (we would be beach-
combers then) (we would be beachdrift)
(we would stick with the contours) (not to
disturb) (what we found there) (not to
erode anything) (not to damage) (what
hasn't been damaged) (any more than it's
already been) (you go undamage something
then) (unbreak it) (unscathe it) (unhex it)

(uncross it) (unharm it) (undemolish some-
thing) (make a countermove) (deploy some-
thing) (makeshift) (something uncertain)
(without any strategies) (no trying to
outmaneuver anything) (without second guess-
ing) (go restore something) (reforest some-
thing) (remind yourself) (have your own
thoughts) (not someone else's) (remind your-
self) (where you stored something) (you might

want to find again) (to give it to someone)
(you might want to keep for later) (not
something) (you go to bazaars for) (not
something) (you find on a rack) (not some-
thing) (you see in a catalog) (as though
through a dim light darkly) (in the pages)
(over the loudspeakers) (inside a seed
catalog) (where you can find complicated
blouses) (and gadgets) (good old time-

savers) (logic monsters) (economical grip-
pers) (rules) (they say we should go by)
(requirements) (things we must have) (as if
that were possible) (who could know so)
(there's nothing to base it on) (it has no
baseline) (nothing to stand on) (no balls)
(to go in or out or over it) (we were near
a very large grandstand) (a whip-cracking
stadium) (a people-pouncing mob was in there)

(they were watching fireworks) (exploding
over and above them) (they were busy) (cel-
ebrating some ancient victory) (their team
was winning) (we were watching) (a great
celebration) (a triumph) (a vindication)
(a mandate) (a result) (of their tenacious
certainty) (they were like giants then)
(we were like seedlings) (we'd just barely
started breathing) (our eyes weren't even open)

(more of you began to be circulating) (into focus)
(you could see yourself in different situations)
(surrounded) (you were still almost always the center)
(from which you looked out) (to try to find someone
you recognized) (who recognized you) (as a kindred)
(nerve center) (as allied) (spur-of-the-moment) (im-
provisions) (could be difficult to manage) (you
weren't managers of much) (you could barely) (manage
to be who you thought you might want to be) (minute

to minute) (your options were more than you'd ever
imagined) (all of a sudden) (you needed a haircut)
(on a particular day) (in a particular style) (that
would be certain) (to give you courage) (consequently
what you wore) (wore you) (out because it was constantly
changing) (and you could look back now) (enough time
had gone by) (there was room to remember) (you were not
the same then) (as you were getting to be now) (who
you were not all that long ago) (seemed remote) (seemed

altogether) (unrelated) (you could wince for who you
were) (you could feel a little pity) (a kind of nostalgia)
(you hadn't run into such an odd feeling) (formerly you
were one gear) (you had no reverse feelings) (to clash
with) (your surroundings were enlarging) (there were
going to be) (more and more layers of circumstances)
(repercussions) (and reverberations) (now and then)
(it gave you the look) (of a laminated headache) (you
arrived and departed simultaneously) (as if you epitomized)

(not knowing if you were coming or going) (managed
to keep those around you) (alerted) (you kept them
off guard) (you specialized in sudden repositioning)
(you were throwing your yokes off) (wrestling away
your splices) (launching yourself) (on unfamiliar ter-
rain) (in search of) (learning another language) (was
hidden inside your everyday one) (you would have to
learn how to find it) (it would take some trial and)
(plenty of error) (to shed from it) (its awkwardness

could turn you into a stranger) (version of yourself
than you'd bargained for) (a little trouble here &
there) (some physical damage) (it was necessary that
you establish a clear understanding) (with all of the
most basic elements) (you and fire had some things to
deal with) (there were chemicals) (that had to be
taken) (to your command station) (for interrogations)
(you were converting) (no longer unquestioning) (done
with asking) (why do you ask) (so many questions)

(we were in question central) (we were bartering) (trying)
(to trade) (to make trades) (we were in question bazaar
territory) (why do you ask) (you ask too many questions)
(if you ask me) (it was a time of terrible tangible
inquisitions) (some splitting of hairs) (tearing-of-
hair time) (some shifting) (some dodging) (very beautiful
evasions) (radiant secrets) (one day a whiff of a witch-
hunt) (one day a sweep of your whole neighborhood) (you
were getting into) (them-and-us-hood) (where many of

the questions wouldn't have to be asked) (they
were settled) (this was a more stable association)
(of like-minded occupants) (who'd recognized one
another) (as having much in common) (and so could
benefit) (from one another's presence) (and enter-
tain) (but not too often) (not necessarily directly)
(an entirely more to the point set of questions)
(severely truncated) (down to the essence) (the
ever alluring) (what's up) (question quintessence)

(you could ransack one another's minds with that one)
(which you did) (on a regular basis) (you were a
talkative people) (all of a sudden) (whispering or
saying or shouting) (for its own sake) (for the
sound effects) (to be uppermost) (these were highly)
(elaborate greeting ceremonies) (carefully circum-
scribed) (rituals of identification) (you could find
affirmation there) (things could be confirmed there)
(you are affirmed, my man) (you have landed in con-

firmation) (lay on the hands) (you have landed) (in
the lap of luxurious magnetic molecules) (everyone's
axis is shimmering) (to tantalize) (to be ceaseless
circulating instable conjunctions) (our red brethren
planet is closer to us) (than they are) (tonight than
it's been for close to 60,000 years) (there won't
be another time) (more years will have to go by)
(circumstantially different) (circles of least con-
fusion to look for) (galaxies of you) (to unleash)

(reservations) (there were so many of them)
(revisions) (whatever suited their needs)
(provisions) (provided in abundance) (kept
hidden) (cables for the bridge) (airshafts
for the tunnels) (ambient air) (without a care
in the world) (all uncluttered) (footloose)
(hard to trace) (impossible to pin down) (on
the move) (in action) (without pity) (pin pity
down) (sore heart) (for such a long drawn-out

sword) (writing's wordless heart beating) (pro-
mise) (virtually) (seamless) (like a coastline)
(very available) (there for the taking) (on prin-
ciple) (by hairline) (air hiding in there) (err
on the side of) (here in there) (ere we meet)
(ere in there) (find us here) (the in there)
(he in her) (her in here) (her in there) (ere
we go) (hat in hand) (knees down) (eyes aside)
(yes in eyes) (leading in pleading) (ending in

lending) (in descending) (order) (an air of con-
clusion) (to the proceedings) (something on the
order) (of a cushioned) (crash landing) (an illu-
sion) (you're moving) (because you aren't) (your
train isn't) (scheduled for departure) (for another
twenty minutes) (went in twenty) (while a train)
(right outside your window) (is slowly leaving)
(you with the sensation) (o in you) (in in minutes)
(you are also leaving) (lo in slow) (motion in a

solution) (to a problem) (rain in train)
(you didn't see coming) (you hadn't been look-
ing) (in the right direction) (eyes misplaced)
(that's your best guess) (what were the odds)
(catalepsy in the casino) (resin resistance)
(a pad foot on casters) (is as in paisley)
(almost too) (intricate) (to follow the swifts)
(down into a chimney) (it's an ancient panto-
graph) (ere we equivocate) (we hesitate) (we

lose) (our bearings) (of good tidings) (fine
driftwood) (quiet shoreline) (mechanical shore-
birds) (print makers) (not one designee) (not
two) (not ten million) (bats under that bridge)
(ere we find paella) (resists jambalaya) (if it
needs to) (if that's what is) (needed) (to fix
what was broken) (and still is) (in need of so
many) (improvements) (come in increments) (almost
unnoticed) (we are too close to them) (to see

almost anything) (that hasn't been) (pointed out
to us) (retrospectively) (settled) (in for the
long haul) (you take the long view) (you were
born there) (you cut your teeth) (in that place)
(it gave you) (an accent) (some stressmarks)
(acute ones) (on the diagonal) (bias cut) (with
gore pleats) (to sway more) (gracefully) (ere
moonlight leaves) (the premises) (are many for
us) (to find one another) (not in another) (for

in former) (lifetimes) (ago) (we were feathers
then) (we were anthers) (we were pistols) (our
smoking guns) (were still smoking) (it was in)
(the time of long shadows) (we made wishes)
(on eyelashes) (our DNA was still smoking) (it
had just been) (taken out) (of the fire) (we
stared into) (as if it would show us) (what we
were made of) (and where we had come from) (to
arrive) (at this juncture) (in these circumstances)

(under these conditions) (at this point) (in
time) (to keep an appointment) (ere an arrow
points in) (many directions) (around the hands)
(on a compass) (om is in there) (ass is) (row
is around) (round is how we go) (there's no way
around that) (it's a fixed bias) (and a bit)
(less awful) (than a straight line) (word stored
in sword) (we stored our provisions) (out of
reach) (of high tide) (away from pandemonium)

(demon in that one) (a very possessive one) (ere
we were demons for) (sticking together) (for the
most part) (we were) (inseparable) (per person)
(one at a time) (we shot back) (in reverse order)
(like swifts from a chimney) (to charm) (there's
no harm) (in there) (one another) (senseless)
(to stare) (at everything) (into one another's
eye secrets) (to see what they were saying) (ere
we close them) (ere flies an arrow out of time)

FIVE

ATTITUDE OF RAGS

It felt like a story sorry it'd lost all its sentences,
Like a sentence looking for its syntax.
All of the words had homeless, unemployed, orphan
Written all over their faces.
It had that parboiled, simmering, half-baked look
Of curiosity about its mouth, like a month of Sundays
Has in the mind of a nonbeliever, a true backslider.
One got the impression reluctance was waxing.
One wanted to say passion was taking a beating.
One wanted to say one's prey to one's feelings.
The feathers of their feelings were all scattered.
It was the kind of day were one to see a flock of
Creepy baby angel heads attached at their necks to
Pitch-black aerodynamically preposterous little wings
Clustering at the sum of things, one would rub one's
Eyes, be too faint to respond, much less explain.
It looked the way a fence looks just after the last
Stampede. A big old blood-colored barn collapsed in
Its tracks. Out of hiding came all the hidden cameras.
It looked like streets look after a parade's disbanded.
It was the kind of day in which emotions roaming from
Town to town, free to be themselves, enjoyed their
Rich fantasy lives. This was the kind of day that day
Was. We were rags in the hands of a narcoleptic duster.

THAT VAGRANT MISTRAL VEXING THE SUN: A FAR CRY

I washed my brain and hung it to dry
In a steady breeze on a black clothesline.
I put a blanket down where it looked as if
The sun would be for a few hours more.
I stood by a long way off, on a tower,
On a rock, on a rooftop made of glass.
I remembered half of bible history in reverse,
I watched myself go back to being a romance
Between two hell-bent cells.
I followed an earthworm as far into its vermiform
Home as it would let me go.
I followed ants carrying nearly invisible separate
Parts of something they wanted to carry back.
I no longer had a face, if I ever did.
The angle of the sun showed me shadows of things
I'd never seen.
I looked at my hands through a magnifying lens
Long enough for smoke to emerge.
I wouldn't need that brain again, I left it
For birds, in lieu of words, and seeds.

INDEPENDENCE DAY

We'd incorporated a laundry lending motion
Detector into the third figure without success.
Everyone commenced dispersing themselves back
To their homes all dejected.
Many fires were set, much ice was cut, a few
Links fell away, a key attached to a braided
Horsehair bracelet got left behind, many more
Samples went into a sample case, midnight unbraided.
Everyone spent the next three days practicing
Free will. They insisted on it. They lived by it.
Was there any other way? That's one thing we wanted
To know. And if there was where would we find it?
Oh, maybe just over there, over the edge of that
Precipice. If no one volunteers we can draw straws.
Everyone spent the next several hours in deep reasoning.
Or at least made it look as if that was what we were
Doing. Then we drew straws to elect a new leader.
Something we suspected not all that pretty was happening
In the cellar. That would have to be saved for later.
We called for a consensus and sure enough we found it.
It looked as if it was perfect. But was it a solution?
Everyone spent the next several days in denial.
Or at least that's what our leader said we were in—
Then we drew straws to elect a new leader.
And sure enough once again it was our old leader who
Drew the shortest straw. And we were back to square one.
But we refused to call it that, we called it progress.
You idiots, our leader said, what have you done with the
Consensus? This caused us every one to become exceedingly
Sheepish. We who'd been so thoroughly entrusted had

Allowed ourselves to be mightily distracted.
Everyone spent the next several months hanging crepe.
That's what our leader said we should do for the rest
Of our lives. So we drew straws to elect a new leader.
No, we set the straw on fire, it started in the cellar,
Old milk cartons, filters, dead animals, it was a
Ghoul's soup down there, and we made up glorious anthems
To praise the courage of our leader.

EARLY-MORNING ECOLOGICAL RADIO

And the ones they wanted most
would have fluorescent orange eyes.
The new bridge would be beautiful,
its cables would be woven by spiders.
Leeches and maggots were back in business
doing for us what they'd always done,
or doing for themselves some things we found
beneficial.
In that life I was held together with hedgehog spine.
Some seeds choose not to germinate for hundreds of
years. That's up to them.
Aren't there some things you wouldn't tell a soul?
It's strange though because you wind up talking to
yourself and there seem to be at least two of you,
sometimes agreeing, sometimes getting into a twisted
bitch. As if you were a kid, back in the wild,
making up a world you sometimes ruled, and sometimes
you had to hide.
When they say one hand isn't telling the other hand
what it's doing, what are they saying? Maybe they're
praying for rain, maybe for rain to go away & rain
somewhere else, it's hard to say.
We tried to bend without buckling & now & then we did.
A past without precedent is the only one it's safe to
visit, we can be one another there without damage, we
can slip into one another's skin.
Pass the garden, please.
We'd spotted a band of insurgent analysands rotating
introspectively into the farm belt.
Once I became accustomed to it, it was good

to have eight legs.
When next we meet I will have sewn for you
a stunningly simple shirt.
As if it were the last living shirt on earth.

THOSE GENERALS' EYES

When I was always the same, someone says,
I was always me. Of course you are, you were,
Someone blurs back, someone shares, as someone
Says, something terrifyingly weird about them-
Selves, something along the lines of if it were up
To me I'd kill us all to spare the pain, not that
Exactly, something worse, something I won't say,
Someone says when I saw them holding hands, says
I wanted to be them then and not be me holding
A different hand, says see, see I looked at who
I was, I saw someone I'd never want to be, some
Of us didn't know what to say, we were speechless,
Our ransacked brains were wild inside their orders,
A full-blooded moon was foaming in our faces.

Now I could see I'd been stirring the pot
For almost ten thousand years.
I could see I'd be stirring forever.
So far nothing'd changed.
Nobody appeared.
I stirred myself into a bottomless sleep,
I was the smallest thing in the world.
Fragment of spit, rumor of mud.
Something that almost might have been.
I no longer had skin or fine hairs along
My arms for wind to chill or an ant to wander
Over. I no longer had friends.
No sister, no brother.
I hadn't cried when my father & my mother
Waved good-bye and their ship exited the harbor.
I hadn't asked them where they were going.
They left me no instructions.

CLAIRSENTIENT GOAT

I wish someone would remind me what happened to my legs,
I can still feel the hand that took me down from the shelf,
I crossed a bridge in the pocket of a coat,
I liked how their music drowned everything out,
For a long time I stayed behind a sugar bowl on a table
Next to a window ledge,
I didn't speak anyone's language,
It took a long time to see all the way down,
Somewhere in the distance there was part of a boat,
I don't know where they went at night,
As if a bottomless body of water were at work,
As if they might never come back,
Sometimes I could watch a woman hoeing,
Some of the trees were covered with leaves,
I felt part of an earthquake, it was very early in the
Morning, I picked up three different warnings,
I couldn't get to the children who were crying,
There was sugar all over the table,
I could hear them under their pillows where they were
Hiding, I wanted my legs back, I asked the ants if
They had seen them before they crossed the river,
I wanted my legs back, I tried to reach the dispatcher
Who stood in a box by the ferry, ants never have
More than one thing on their minds,
Note on a wave, one drop of blood, one leg at a time,
I can feel the hand that put me down on this ledge.

FAUX SELF-PORTRAIT OF YOU

You are a very uneven person.
You, on the other hand, the one with not quite
five fingers, are a very uneven person.
Look me in the eye I say with conviction and say
you are a person of complete unevenness.
I look away to look for the surface of something
whose unevenness is its main attraction.
Very uneven person, I address you haphazardly,
you are a patchy, jerky lurcher.
You are nonuniform. You are subsubsubstantial,
I say to you of the fluctuating essence of uneven-
ness. No, I say, I am not a triangle, I do not
fit in the corner. I am an uneven piece of furn-
iture. There is a sirocco in you today.
You are a difficult table. Anything that rolls
rolls off of you almost immediately.
You're not good for a broken string of beads,
Is this not so I say uneven person that you are.
I look down to watch the beads roll where the floor
leans. An odd lullaby passes through my hair.

INCIDENT ON THE ROAD TO THE CAPITAL

A wolf had grown tired of his character and sought
to find a means to transform himself into something
more vicious, more deadly. While his coat was slick,
thick and well colored, for he was an excellent hunter,
he yearned for something to do that had nothing to do
with survival or instinct. He no longer killed because
he needed to or could. All that was useless, too practical,
too obvious. He wanted to kill for some other purpose.
For all of his successfully completed kills, his perfect
record of stealth and elusion, he felt nothing. When he
ran into me the other day on his journey to consult the
oracle of escalated suffering we shared a table in the
shade of a parasol tree in whose branches were preening
half a dozen or so birds with gaudy chromatic feathers.
A few of these fell onto the dome of his forehead but he
was too engrossed in his story to brush them away. He
didn't look like a very serious wolf. I think he was
missing a real opportunity.

PROSE POEM

For a long time I'd wanted to be in a prose
poem and could find no way to do so that
I despaired I'd ever get to but here I am now
and I will not leave here until my desire to
be in a prose poem is satisfied and so I will
not stray out of this prose poem even while
I don't know what to do in here and though I'm
lost when it comes to what could or should be
happening in this prose poem I will take up a
digression that involves a crazy essay recently
read about what hideous prisons paragraphs are
and how until writers find new ways around them
paragraphs will hold writers hostage and never
let them think thoughts other than thoughts para-
graphs delimit with their omnipotent paragraph
authority. So there. I'm feeling just fine now
sticking around in this prose poem giving me
a very satisfying prose poem feeling and perhaps
some time later long after I've exited this
prose poem I can look back with nostalgic poign-
ancy thanking and praising the prose poem for
allowing me to spend a short time in its precincts.
I'm now leaving this prose poem.

IT WASN'T EXACTLY LIKE BEING LEFT STANDING
AT THE ALTAR

I had on my superfine handy translation glasses
So I could see what you mean.
It was worth selling my soul for
The convenience.
To memorize comes about as easily to me as a mouse
Comes to a cat. But some things I remember.
It was a memorable evening.
So I closed my eyes and spun the globe but it
Was one of those perpetual-motion globes, filled
With indecision, with minds of its own.
Remember when I told you about the memory competitions?
Remember how I made my fortune?
Once I wrote a novel & it was made into a movie &
The movie won an Oscar & licensing & franchises
Were gravy.
You remember the story?
At first I wouldn't take any money.
A sinister but lovable band of pranksters with too
Much time on their hands plot to steal everything
From out of all the time capsules there are in the world.
Nothing's too insignificant or unambitious.
They succeed. They go undetected. It's a perfect
Crime. The movie's just a lot of dialogue with them
Sitting around in a condemned movie house arguing
About what to do next.
Beats me. You're the one who left me with all that
Time to kill. No dubbing, no subtitles, that's
All I remember about the contract.
What am I telling you this for, you were my agent.

THE SHADOWS

To be like a spider a kid's captured
In a bug house and forgotten on a bench
Beneath a room inside a hemlock in the far-off
Corner of a garden, then it's raining
Someone simmering
Someone sleeping in an airplane flying over the Atlantic
Flyway
We looked at a map dotted with fires and reached
For a pencil to draw lines between them to see if
A figure might emerge into which some kind of meaning
Might be assigned
There was a whooping crane for whom we'd wept
With a fish in its mouth, frowning
There was an endless chain-link fence
To be like a vine finding a fence a good enough home
To be a scrap of foil someone's fashioned into a bird
Or what passes for a bird made of foil
Every time you think of me I shudder, why else
Would I stay inside the shadows
Why else would I step aside
You were the one who asked me more than once what
Is it that makes something make sense
I think you wore that thought out until it was worn
The way a blanket a child uses to find how sleep shows
What sleep does
To be fooled with inside a perpetual-motion shuffling
Of cards, to be folded like a paper fan, to be used
To cool a face, to be clipped to spokes on a wheel
Now you tell me how sound travels as you throw a
Replica of my head over a rail into a river
It was about time. I needed to know how some thing

Worked
I liked how you made my head out of an old cannonball
I liked how you made my eyes look tired
I liked the expression of mild disbelief
You put on my face
I liked the color you used and where you put the arrows
I liked flying through the air like an arrow
I liked how you stole the cannonball from a battery
In a rainstorm in the summertime
Once we hid in a gunnery on a precipice far away
From everything
Once you let me pick what color leaves would be
Sometimes you didn't care what I was thinking
Or what my hands were up to
Or you asked me what was on my mind and there was
Nothing I could say
To be soundproof, to not breathe a word
Like water trickling through a sand trap inside a cistern
Like a seed inside an envelope inside an icebox
Like a bandage folded on a workbench
Like something someone hands you you put inside your
Pocket
It's good you didn't tell me what was on the horizon
It took a long time though eventually I began to under-
Stand why you stayed away from fortune-tellers and
Speculators of all kinds
They always gave me the whammies
They always gave me the shivers
Once someone sent me uninvited my complete astro-
Logical chart
It felt on my back as if a sharpshooter had me in

His line of sight, as if I were rightly stalked
Don't worry, I didn't read it
I sent it back
I remember the time you loaned me your scarf
I remember the morning a ghost in a cocktail dress
Walked past us on a freezing strand of beach
I remember when you did or didn't part your hair
I remember what happened to your eyes
I liked how you made them two zeros
I liked how you made them two galaxies
I watched the way you could cross them
You were the one with the knapsack and boat
The one with dirt on your shoes and dust on your
Shoulders
I was the one with a glass of cool water

SOME NOT SO NEARLY APOCALYPTIC BORDERS
IN THE ANTIPODES

It begins with a broad idea about not being there,
It's tied to a string disappearing beneath
The surface water of a crooked river, a river
Working overtime to make itself straight and deeper,
Maybe deep enough to slice a whole ball of worms
In half, the kind of worms it's okay to do that to,
Since it accelerates their means of reproduction,
Or so it says somewhere in a scout's notebook
Including a lot of other weird rationalizations,
Some time-saving schemes, really simple recipes,
But mainly seems to have as its central focus
A rash theology of the tying and untying of knots,
But not too many of them are left, they went the way
Of all good scouts, god rest their souls, suppose
X is here thinking thinking thinking about Y there
Most likely sleeping dreaming of X thinking of Y
Dreaming of fishing, it's written somewhere in a book,
Fishing in water addles the brain, 10 years later,
There not being an idea abroad it begins beneath,
Disappears that string, it is tied to a river,
Deeper and straight itself to make over time, working
Worms to slice enough deep maybe to that to do okay
It's worms of the kind reproduction notebook in a
Scout's somewhere it says rationalizations, recipes,
Simple really, schemes time-saving some focus
Central it's as to have seems mainly knots of untying
And tying of theologies rash the way they went,
Left of them are many too not but suppose their souls,
Rest god, scouts good, all of there Y about thinking,
Thinking here is X, Y of X thinking, of dreaming

Sleeping most likely in a book somewhere written
It's fishing of dreaming later years, 10, the brain
Addles water, it begins with a broad idea about not
Being there, the river disappears around the bend,
There's insanity in the marketplace, in the grocery
Aisles, there are egrets feeding fish to their babies
In the Atchafalaya cypress groves.

WAS

That was before there was no way to get to
The other side without going the long way around,
We hadn't yet begun to take ourselves apart,
Oil was just beginning to know what it was,
Was wasn't yet set in its matrix,
I saw tomorrow fixed on a star, on a barge,
Courage, someone said, was all the rage,
That was before we'd come to the cutting edge,
The other side might be the other side of a door,
We hadn't yet finished half of what we started,
Oil was just burning over alphabets & mending,
Was was no stranger than night-blooming jasmine,
We hadn't yet begun to know half of what we wanted,
There wasn't any difference between what we started
Or we finished, or so said our new circular arguments

A THOUSAND WORDS

An appendix, four wisdom teeth, tonsils:
In case one journeys into chasms without doctors
It will just make things simpler in the future
You will appreciate ice cubes more   29
A public scandal, a private investigation, no clue:
It rocks foundations upon which sleepiness naps
How to find a way to appear to not be asking questions
No, ask no questions, no, ask magnificent questions
For whose answers there won't be anything anyone
Anticipated much less imagined   76
Something tonic for the fugue, automatic for the
Anatomic organic paraparadise paraparallel annexes,
Unbony for knees, like socks fit a rooster like they
Say in the boonies to start the anagogic ceremonies,
Please, baby, please turn the allegorical fires down
By a few degrees, the head on my hair's beginning
To burn   128
And there's no
Need to get down on
All fours
Gruesome
Reasons though there
Are
Needing picking up off the floor?   149
I liked to watch them changing horses in midstream
At dusk, in autumn, after leaves no longer allemanded
At midnight, in moonlight, in untinted movies,
In an unheated room, under chilly white flowers,
Lamia all over the map was what Heidelberg said,
Denizens widespread, bevels everywhere, fast-
Breaking fascicles & a prayer for equilibrium,   202

They bent their brows up and down over true-blue
Palimpsest water troughs where their fathers and
Their mothers had left them little love notes: 226
Be good to the wolves
There's something behind the stones, back of the
Stove
We're sorry we called the malarial marsh The Vale
Of Health
We're sorry we couldn't afford to keep the horse
Watch out for anything called a long leash
We put some things aside, in the tin box, in the
Leather case, behind the radiator
And check between the drive shaft & the muffler   293
I remember you with wind all over your face
I remember you with snow all over your nose
I remember what your puzzled look wouldn't let on
I remember your comb
I remember fourscore places you signed your name
I remember two different handwritings you used
I remember a coat you threw off of a cliff
I remember the colors you couldn't see
I remember our initials on a roadside table   364
Once you dove into a lake in the middle of the night
And you were gone so long we thought you were never
Coming back
We were questioning the motives of the motives
And had to slap ourselves to get over it and
Get it over with   411
An edict: make a run for it
Someone decided that hall of the sports teams
Would be required to give us back our colors

One by one in tip-top condition
Several ceremonies involved dove release activity
The birds aren't actually given a choice
I don't know where they go
The photographic record's drama is heightened
Smart as a whip, sharp as a tack   474
It was a given
They'd look immediately into the closet
They were warned not to open
Without fail a dream entomologist bursts into
My dreams to collect insects of various kinds
And then he leaves and the dream goes on   514
Some of them countenanced an unacceptably
Rational relationship with mortality
Some of us freaked out over it
So we had a few screws loose but we were all there
We didn't get rabid about it
When we hallucinated we hallucinated as one   556
I remember you with your head thrown back, with
Burning leaves making you laugh
I remember you under a live oak holding a glass
I remember what mattered in your palace of memory
I remember what happened to the soles of your shoes
You were the one who taught me every last hydraulic
Thing   610
The dog brown fox jumped quick over the lazy
The the
Once in a
A laminated blue moon
Nobody stopped me from writing two names on
Paper slips and throwing them into a fire   644

Nobody told me to leave the suitcases alone
You know what they say where we live, if you don't
Like the buzzwords stick around, get out of the
Kitchen
Anticloning indexes were off the charts those
Days
As if
As luck would have it
As if who knew
As soon as we have half a chance   700
At this time, more than ever, in countless ways
I'm sorry I put a locket in my shoe and let a
Sailor steal it
I'm sorry I lied about where I lost my wallet
I'm sorry every last text isn't sacred   741
It was good sleeping on a pallet overnight in
The open air in the market
I liked it when I couldn't figure from where the
Music was coming
It was good sweeping a sidewalk at 5 in the morning
Just as rain showers stopped   785
Who was it you wanted to see one last time
Which was the one they cut out of the picture
What's the name of that little town in the Pyrenees
We were fired up for a good illusion   823
We had sometimes driven one another mad
On the other hand
Sometimes we drove one another on missions of
Mercy
I meant what I said when I paused over our being
At the mercy of a chemistry of infinite numbers

But you know I don't know what I mean 872
Let's talk about the butterfly with crimson red
Expandable wings, eight of them
I liked watching a boy try on clothes he knew
No longer fit him 899
I remember a grown man so small he broke the
Mold
Is the one-legged bird lucky to be alive
One of them asked what made words flying out
Of a mouth make sense 932
One of them had painted blue numbers on a black
Mailbox
One of them had driven straight into a fence
In daylight, cold sober, uncomprehending
In the picture a soldier is dreaming in chron-
Ological order of all of our previous wars
In the picture seven forces are meeting at the
Crossroad in broad daylight
Some the churches wouldn't have were buried at
The crossroad as if it would 1000

INDEX OF TITLES AND FIRST LINES

BIBLIOGRAPHY

BLOOD, HOOK & EYE (University of Texas Press, 1977)
She Has This Phantom Limb, The Direction to the Left of Sunrise

ALL YOU HAVE IN COMMON (Carnegie Mellon University Press, 1984)
The Dark Side of the Moon, A Graphic Map of Eternity, Colorless Green
Ideas

BLUE FOR THE PLOUGH (Carnegie Mellon University Press, 1992)
Still in Wonder, Hypnagogic, Life Based on a Worthless Dare, Tvi, A
Handful of Porcupine Quills, Longing, Winslow Homer's Blues

OUR MASTER PLAN (Carnegie Mellon University Press, 1999)
Little Black Tangrams, Daytrip to Paradox, The White Boat, Apology
for and Further Explanation of an Attempt to Divert Accusations of
Equivocation, 5½ Inch Lullaby, Interview, Fly on the Wall, Don't Say My
Name, Untitled, A Secret Life, I Remember Rilke, After the Birds Learned
to Count to Eight, Company, Our Master Plan, All in a Day's Work, The
Soup Drill, Without a Similar Condition Including This Condition

VOYAGES IN ENGLISH (Carnegie Mellon University Press, 2001)
If I Were a Raptor Cruising through the Timetables of History, Is It You?,
One Enchanted Evening, A Caged-In Exposition of Conceptions Evolved in
Logic and Words: a love story, Thief of Sparks, On the Ownership of Time,
A Peep of Saints, Hidden Assets, After the Car Museum, Against All Odds,
For a Few Seconds There I Was a Panther, Catholic, Gullible Mosquito,
Tribute to Charles Darwin for Someone Else, Astronomy Lake, A Trailing-
Off of Arguments in Prospect of Laments in the Graveyard of Unfinished
Things, The Next Step, Perhaps Died & Gone to Heaven, A Personal Essay:
a personal wish to fall down, A Modern Version of the Way the Rosary Was
Once Said throughout Western Europe in the Late Middle Ages

HAT ON A POND (Verse Press, 2001)

Balsam of Myrrh, Last Syllable of Recorded Time, Awe of Everything, Sea Foam, An Error Lurks in Such a Certainty, Endless Afternoons in a Spring Ice Storm on Mountain Roads in the Poconos, Fugue Pirogue on Bayou St. John, Precious Celestial Membrane, Fear of Psychic Surgery, Contrast of Blues with an Element of Orange in the Golden Bronze of Corn, Instances of Wasted Ingenuity, Wishing There Were Some Better Ways of Explaining Ourselves to Birds, The Great Divide, Twisted, Fucked-Up, Poor Excuse, Hot Pursuit of the Unapproachable, Soul Migration, More Than We Knew What to Do With, Summertime, Nightshade, Paradisiac, Nine Sunflowers Standing Seven Feet High Wintering Over in a Snowy Field, She Thinks She Hung the Moon, Not That Lake, Borderline Case of Insubstantial Vacillating Breakfast Suspense, Romantic, Edges in Creases, A Walk Up the Even and Down the Odd Sides of a Street, Cord of Wood, Spark of Shoes, Good Detective, Tame Swans, A Tango We Negotiated to Turn Our Train Around, The Cold War, Idiographic

REVERSE RAPTURE (Verse Press, 2005)

prologue: *a stick, a cup, a bowl, a comb; that was a cove, that was an inlet; domain of a hidden evening; show some compassion; reverse rapture; a rest from forced marches; instant justice; against interpretation; emancipated; x in fix*

REMNANTS OF HANNAH (Wave Books, 2006)

Attitude of Rags, That Vagrant Mistral Vexing the Sun: a far cry, Independence Day, Early-Morning Ecological Radio, Those Generals' Eyes, For a Chinese Poet Writing through the Night Up on the Edge of Mt. Pollux, Clairsentient Goat, Faux Self-Portrait of You, Incident on the Road to the Capital, Prose Poem, It Wasn't Exactly like Being Left Standing at the Altar, The Shadows, Some Not So Nearly Apocalyptic Borders in the Antipodes, Was, A Thousand Words